Experience the experience
of the experience!

L.U.A.

Bill Mc Grane

IN CELEBRATION OF UNIQUENESS

A tribute to William (Bill) McGrane who left this mortal world on
October 14, 1991 and yet left some of him with each who knew him.

A blossom has fallen in God's garden. And in its separation from its floral home we, who gazed at and enjoyed its beauty, stand in wonder as we contemplate the void. Our memories are kindled. Our emotions stoked. And each, in his or her own way, relives those joyous moments in which God's gift to us enriched our lives.

God gave us our senses of touch, smell, taste, sight and sound. Yet somehow this lover of life found a way to extend each:
- Morsels became banquets
- Words were music to the soul
- Experiences viewed as opera
- And—Embraces became the touchstone of relationships.

God used his messenger well. We came to know in simple truths the universal plan. Where each human was destined for uniqueness, to love and be loved. And—all experiences, painful and otherwise, became steps on the ladder of life taking us ever forward and upward.

We are grateful for his presence as he modeled for us the plan of self enrichment:
- Affirm the unaffirmed
- Eliminate value judging
- Feed your mind
- Speak with gentleness
- Listen with your heart
- Turn anger to love
- And remember, each of us in all we do are ever doing the best we can.

Thank you God for Bill McGrane, though we are separated physically, we are eternally bonded. His word, his style, his sensitivity is sealed in the memory bank of all who knew him. His celebration of life is part of our history. We will think of him often, in special ways which each of us call memories. Father, husband, brother, son, uncle, grandfather, cousin, friend, associate, counselor, teacher, mentor—all names to define the distinctiveness of our special relationship.

A blossom has fallen in God's garden. God has taken the earthly form of William McGrane. Yet we, who celebrate his life, believe that even now the angels celebrate. For in his coming, the spirit, the uniqueness of this unusual man, brightens his heavenly home. Thank You God for his visit and thank you Bill for the special gift of you.

Love and T.U.A.
Dave Yoho
October 17, 1991

Glowing comments from corporate, entrepreneurial, sales, marketing, speaking, educational, government and other leaders about. . . .

Brighten Your Day With Self-Esteem
by William J. McGrane, CPAE

"I say without reservation that I have never known a greater 'human engineer' than my friend Bill McGrane. As founder and Chairman Emeritus of The National Speakers Association, I know many speakers and writers, and Bill McGrane is among those at the top. We are most grateful for his contribution with this book."

Cavett Robert
Founder and Chairman Emeritus of
The National Speakers Association

"Our society is filled with people striving for what others think they 'should' be, rather than enjoying what and who they are. *Brighten Your Day With Self-Esteem* is THE manual for a happier and more fulfilling life, and a celebration of who you are. Businesses, schools and families will benefit from the skills taught, and the love shared. Bill McGrane teaches us how better to respect ourselves and others around us. Our world needs more people who live by the lessons and principles shared in this wonderful book."

Jay Rifenbary
President of the Rifenbary Training and Development Center
Author of *No Excuse!*

"This is the best book on Self-Esteem I have ever read. I'll re-read it and share it at every opportunity."

Charlie "Tremendous" Jones, CPAE
Speaker and Bestselling Author of *Life Is Tremendous*

"Bill McGrane's 'big hug-print' is now a part of planet Earth. Most of the members of my family have been through the McGrane Self-Esteem Institute. Each of our lives reflects this great man. The gems contained in this volume are timeless! And could be lifesavers."

Ty Boyd, CPAE
Speaker and Consultant

"If you knew Bill McGrane, as I did, you can hear his voice, his wisdom on every page of *Brighten Your Day With Self-Esteem*. If you didn't have the privilege of knowing Bill, you *will* after reading this book! *Brighten Your Day* is important, effective and all-McGrane. My thanks to all those who are keeping Bill's work alive."

Jim Tunney, EdD, CSP, CPAE
Former NFL Referee

"A wealth of practical, wise formulas to put into life application. The product of an incredible man's mind, soul and living."

Naomi Rhode, CSP, CPAE
Vice President of Smart Practice
Immediate Past President of
The National Speakers Association

"My life changed dramatically as a result of the skills and knowledge gained through my relationship with Bill McGrane and the information contained in his book! In 1980 I was unemployed and on the verge of giving up on life itself. I went from eating peanut butter and crackers to owning and operating my own training and consulting practice. We are internationally recognized as the cutting edge of automotive sales skills. Using Bill's Self-Esteem and communication principles helped me create quantum leaps in success and happiness for over 70,000 retail automotive people around the world. You too can have similar changes and accomplishments. Read this book and use the information and ideas. Taking action is the key! As Bill said, 'Do these things and then watch what happens.'"

Ken Petty
President of K-P Consulting

"Bill McGrane helped me through a tough political life-and-death time in my life. I was challenged with staying alive in my business and Bill knew how to 'go-right-to-the-core-of-the-matter.' This book can help you get to the core and handle issues in a practical, simple manner. You can refer to this book often for solutions to life issues."

Nick Carter, CSP, CPAE
Nightingale-Conant Corporation

"Bill McGrane was a gifted teacher, a sensitive mentor and a loyal friend. I was blessed when our paths crossed. He opened my eyes, challenged my mind and touched my heart. Read this book and your paths will cross!"

Suzy Sutton, CSP
Speaker, Trainer, Entertainer

"Bill McGrane dedicated his life to the issues of self-esteem. His work, as embodied in *Brighten Your Day*, is a prescription for much of the malaise within society today. If you seek a monument to Bill McGrane, you will find it within the words, thoughts and ideas in this book."

Dave Yoho, CPAE
Consultant, Speaker & Video Trainer
Author of *How To Have A Good Year Every Year*

"What a valuable resource! Bill McGrane inspired so many through his work and his life—and now, a treasure for all times to be read, studied and enjoyed."

Nido R. Qubein, CSP, CPAE
Creative Services, Inc.
Past President, National Speakers Association

"As my mentor for too short a time, Bill McGrane taught me how to reach into myself to find the foundation for what I do. He possessed an uncanny ability to help people reach and exceed their potential. His book reflects and provides that energy so Bill McGrane's legacy can make a difference for future generations. I only wish I could get a personally autographed copy!"

Roger Herman, CSP, CMC
Business Futurist, Management Consultant, Speaker
Author of *Turbulence!*

"A life of true joy and happiness, the kind of life our Creator has in mind for us, is possible *only* when we possess a proper sense of our own self-esteem. What is so very important to realize is that we control that sense of self-esteem. Self-esteem needs to be worked at every day for the rest of our lives as it deteriorates. That's the glory of *Brighten Your Day With Self-Esteem*—a powerful, practical handbook for daily control of self-esteem. I strongly suggest this is a book for everyone, for a lifetime."

Fr. Bob Hunt
Member of the National Speakers Association

"Bill McGrane has come alive on the pages of this book! His words reflect the wisdom and questioning skills of Socrates, delivered with the gentleness of a fawn. Read this book, take action on Bill's self-esteem ideas, 'then watch what happens.'"

Elizabeth Jeffries, CSP
Author of *The Heart of Leadership*

"Everyone needs to read this book to learn and live its wisdom. Bill McGrane took the place of my deceased father as a mentor. He helped me learn to communicate with people to reach mutually beneficial outcomes. The self-esteem principles in this book will help you develop in-depth, meaningful, lasting, personal and professional relationships. In the networking business, which is people helping people, these principles were essential in helping Linda and me build a multi-million dollar worldwide distribution business."

Russ and Linda Karlen
NuSkin/Interior Design Nutritionals
Hawaiian Blue Diamond Executives

"This book is a collection of a life's work. Not just the life of Bill McGrane, but of the thousands of lives he helped, that he enhanced with his messages and that he saved with his philosophies of total and unconditional love and acceptance. I became a student of Bill's in September 1974. He profoundly and permanently changed my life with his powerful ideas, as contained in this book. His beliefs can help you too, however only if you are wanting and willing to change."

Jim Pancero
Professional Speaker and Sales Trainer

"Bill McGrane saved my life when I didn't have the vision or stamina to go on. I went from frenzied to harmonious living. He stretched out his hands through the Art of Asking Questions to help ME find MY path. This was his normal behavior as he helped many a heart travel from self-absorption and panic to honest, healthy caregiving. Bill McGrane was a world master teacher. Everyone that came in contact with him still carries his energy of enlightenment. I'm so sure that everyone who touches this book will be blessed with the same. However, be warned: when you read this book, you will be forever changed with the inability to stand in ignorance because once you know you cannot NOT know."

Lois Jacobini
President
Jacobini Associates

"WOW. . . . Have you ever wanted to have a grandfather, father, master mentor or great teacher to have heart to heart discussions with you? Then you discover your life direction and future were more clear. This volume cuts to the core issues of life and captures the essence of William J. McGrane's love, wisdom, layered questions and deeply impacting way. P.S. Every page required a capital 'NB' for nota bene or note well!"

Bill Cantrell, CSP
Cantrell Training and Consulting
Customized Values-Centered Training

"Every now and then someone who has a captivating personality, is very articulate and is a professional in selling ideas, experiences a magnificent 'Aha!' breakthrough. Bill McGrane was one of those very special people. He discovered the awesome power of self-esteem and dedicated his life to helping people understand it, enhance it in themselves and give it to others. The title of this book is a perfect fit. If you can no longer *Brighten Your Day* by spending time with Bill McGrane you can *certainly* do so with this priceless collection of his wisdom and guidance. Thanks Bill for one more gigantic positive gift to the people who want to become what they can be!"

Jim Newman, CPAE
Creator of the PACE seminars
Bestselling Author of *Release Your Brakes!*

"Bill McGrane wrote it down and spoke it so thousands could understand we can choose the direction of our lives. Now there is an opportunity for all of us to take those words and energize and re-energize our lives."

W. Mitchell, CSP, CPAE
Motivational speaker on "Taking Responsibility For Change"
Author of *The Man Who Won't Be Defeated*

Leaders' comments continued on page 220 . . .

BRIGHTEN YOUR DAY WITH SELF-ESTEEM

How to Empower, Energize & Motivate Yourself to a Richer, Fuller, More Rewarding Life

WILLIAM J. McGRANE, CPAE

A Success Publishers Book
Published by Markowski International Publishers
Hummelstown, PA USA

Brighten Your Day With Self-Esteem
William J. McGrane, CPAE

Copyright © 1995 by McGrane Self-Esteem Institute

Published by Success Publishers
Markowski International Publishers
One Oakglade Circle
Hummelstown, PA 17036 USA
Success Publishers is an imprint and trademark of
Markowski International Publishers

Edited by Miriam Burkart and Mike and Marjie Markowski
Manufactured in the United States of America

Publisher's Cataloging in Publication
(Prepared by Quality Books, Inc.)

McGrane, William J. (1925–1991)
Brighten your day with self-esteem: how to empower, energize & motivate yourself to a richer, fuller, more rewarding life /
   William J. McGrane, CPAE — 1st ed.
   p. cm. — (Personal development series)
   Preassigned LCCN: 94-078261.
   ISBN 0-938716-21-2 (Cloth)
   ISBN 0-938716-20-4 (Paper)

1. Self-esteem.   2. Success—Psychological aspects.   3. Self-realization.
I. Title BF697.5.S46M34 1995
                                                                    158'.1
                                                              QBI94-2375

Dedication

This book is dedicated to my wife, Dean Bowman McGrane, for her support, love, belief in me and Total Unconditional Acceptance.

About the Author

William J. McGrane, CPAE was the founder of the McGrane Self-Esteem Institute. He was an internationally known and recognized public speaker, seminar facilitator, and Self-Esteem consultant.

He began his career at the age of 24 as assistant superintendent of schools, as well as purchasing and contracting officer for the Antilles Consolidated Schools—Federal Security Agency in Puerto Rico. When he returned to the States he turned a hotel/athletic club into a great success by increasing membership from 250 to 2500. Bill also owned a catering service, gourmet shop and restaurant.

Bill was vice president of a New York Stock Exchange firm for 14 years. He became the top Mutual Fund salesman and was the training director for the First Columbus Corporation. He won numerous sales awards and introduced the concept of buying term insurance and investing the difference in mutual funds.

Because of his business success, Bill was asked to teach Orientation To Business at the University of Cincinnati. The University President, Dr. Warren Bennis, recognized Bill as an outstanding, innovative and creative teacher.

In 1978, Bill received the CPAE (Council of Peers Award for Excellence) from the National Speakers Association, a designation conferred for excellence in public speaking, including such luminaries as Dr. Norman Vincent Peale, Richard DeVos, Ty Boyd, Charlie "Tremendous" Jones and Ronald Reagan. Bill also received the Ohio Governor's Award for Community Action.

He was a pioneer in the field of Self-Esteem. For over 49 years, Bill did qualitative research on how Self-Esteem affects relationships and career. Bill was an eclectic learner, a wordsmith and a master teacher. He created, developed and presented a two day *Self-Esteem Program* and a five day personal and professional life style program called *Psycho-Linguistics*.

Bill was unique because of his vast experience and leadership positions in Education, Hotel and Club Management, Investment Banking, Insurance, and Human Resource Development. His Socratic style of speaking and teaching created a learning atmosphere where people invested deeply in ownership and application of knowledge and information.

He died of pancreatic cancer on October 14, 1991. Bill can best be described by a poem he wrote in his personal journal on April 6, 1983:

Every day I have the time
To give a person something sublime
As people share their pain with me
My outcome is to—set them free.

Acknowledgments

In reviewing his life and how others have touched and impacted William J. McGrane, CPAE, the following people need to be thanked. Their influence on Bill helped make this book possible.

To Bill's parents, Agnes and William McGrane, Sr., for their love and nurturing. To his sister, Margaret McGrane Winters, for an agreement they made as young children that taught him commitment and discipline. To his sister, Rita McGrane Homan, for teaching Bill how to give himself away and for her nurturing.

He constantly spoke of two teachers who believed in him long before he believed in himself—thank you, Sister Xavier and Sister Marie Bernadette.

Dean McGrane, Bill's wife, needs to be acknowledged for knowing it when she saw it! Through her love and devotion, she gave Bill what he needed at each stage of his development. Their relationship reaches beyond this physical world—it has also been spiritual. She is truly Bill's soul mate.

A special thank you to Bill's four children: Joan McGrane Cutlip for her affirming ways; Kit McGrane Petricone for her elegant sensitivity; Bill McGrane III for his desire, congruence and his skill of creating balance; Bob McGrane for his child-likeness, creativity and acceptance.

An individual who supported Bill as he added to his business knowledge was Ned Barthalmus, of The First Columbus Corporation.

Thank you, Larry Wilson, for your influence on Bill by introducing him to your ideas and Abraham Maslow. He always appreciated your friendship.

Chris Hagerty is acknowledged for his friendship, openness and giving Bill a gold mine when he lead Bill to L. S. Barksdale.

Bill was forever grateful to L.S. Barksdale, of the Barksdale Foundation, for helping him discover his missing piece, thus finding freedom.

Two of Bill's favorite mentors were Socrates and Abraham Maslow. Thank you for BEING you and contributing to mankind. These men modeled the pioneering spirit.

Thank you to Miriam Burkart for her 15 years of dedication in working with Bill as he laid the foundation for and built the McGrane Self-Esteem Institute. Your tireless efforts in assembling the "Brighten Your Day" messages and getting them into publishing form are much appreciated.

A special thank you to Hersch Wilson for his input and recommendation on several key issues.

Linda Combs is appreciated for her final edit and proofreading of the manuscript.

A hearty thank you to Mike and Marjie Markowski for editing the manuscript and publishing the book. Their work, persistence and determination helped make this book possible.

Finally, an enormous Thank You to every graduate of all of the programs that Bill facilitated. You energized him to BE the best he could BE! Because of you—Bill was fulfilled!

Contents

Foreword

In the winter of 1995 I was asked to write a foreword to *Brighten Your Day With Self-Esteem*, a book of lessons, anecdotes and affirmations on Self-Esteem written over a lifetime by the late Bill McGrane, a man for whom I had much esteem. I thought, "I can do that. I've been speaking and writing about Self-Esteem for almost thirty years."

So I began mulling it over, thinking about insightful stories and quotable quotes.

About that same time, I gave a speech to a corporate client; I've been speaking to groups like this for thirty years. The only difference was this speech truly and completely bombed. I *felt* disjointed; I wasn't making any sense and the audience gave me feedback that pretty much reinforced my evaluation. God forbid, no one even laughed at my jokes—that is the ultimate knife in the chest for someone who makes their living making speeches. I *felt* terrible, I *felt* like my career was over. I *felt* that the only occupation left for me was stumbling around in my garden examining rocks. If I was lucky, my dogs would still like me!

So much for my Self-Esteem.

On the airplane going home, I thought, "I don't know anything about Self-Esteem. I just want to go home and go to bed." It's a funny thing how life works. When we get a little cocky and full of ourselves, it has a way of knocking us up-side-the-head with a "two-by-four." The "wake-up call" to me was that Self Esteem isn't a glib, to be taken lightly, subject. It is, for all of us, a critically important part of who we are. It is not something we can just presume. It is something we need to work on every day. No matter how successful or experienced we are, we are all vulnerable, if we choose to be, to life's little "wake-up calls."

So I went home, into my little studio. I thought about Self-Esteem and wrote down the first words that came to mind:

uniqueness	*perspective*
acceptance	*truth*
humor	

When I think of people I've met in my life who have Self-Esteem, the first thing that springs to mind is that they believe they are *unique* and valuable human beings. From that core belief springs much. They trust their opinions, their beliefs and their sense of ethics. They are not easily swayed from what they believe is right, especially what they believe is right for them.

Next, they *accept* themselves, warts and all, imperfections and out-and-out character flaws. They are working on all of the above, yet at the same time, they *accept* the fact that they are "fallible human beings" and always will be.

Self-Esteem individuals learn not to take themselves too seriously and to keep their lives in *perspective*. God knows, there are awful, terrible and truly serious matters that we all need to attend to in our lives. However, we often act as if everything is serious, i.e., that work and making money are serious. Most importantly, we may bamboozle ourselves into thinking we are "serious people" and everyone else "should" pay attention and homage to us (this is our ego speaking). We "make up" the idea that if we are not always right, if we don't always win, if we ever look foolish or ridiculous, or feel uncomfortable, we will somehow be diminished. We walk around in our power suits, to our power meetings. We get angry when we get stuck in traffic, and we take ourselves very seriously.

Keeping perspective means being tied into the rhythm of life and the symphony of movement between the serious and the comical, between the poignant moments holding your new-born child in your arms for the first time and the moments of utter boredom. Keeping perspective means we rarely take ourselves too seriously, even when we are doing serious work or serious play.

Finally, when I think of Self-Esteem, I also think of *truth;* of relentlessly telling the truth to ourselves. The individuals I have come across in my life who have Self-Esteem are masters at the simple, yet difficult "art of truth teliing."

The picture that sticks in my mind is of the Roman conquerors as they came back to Rome from their wars of conquest, in a caravan of riches won to the cheering of the crowd. The Roman generals would have a slave at their right shoulder whispering in their ear, "This is all illusion." Kahlil Gibran, the Lebanese poet, wrote that we need to treat triumph and tragedy as the same impostor. Telling the truth to ourselves means seeing the difference between who we really are and everything else. We are unique and fallible beings; there is nothing like us in the universe! Who we are springs solely from this fact, nothing else. Everything else is external and not "who we are." The praise, adulation, criticism, college degrees, job, car, house, failures and our clothes are all illusions. They are impostors; they are not who we are. Telling the truth to ourselves means being able to tell the difference.

When you put all of this together; a belief in your innate *uniqueness*, self-*acceptance*, *perspective*, a lot of *humor* and the ability to tell the *truth* to yourself, the result is Self-Esteem.

We need to work on it every day. We need to know how to talk to ourselves every day. We all talk to ourselves. When I speak about talking to ourselves in the workshops we teach, I start by asking, "How many people talk to themselves?" Most hands in the group go up. Yet there are always a few people who keep their arms crossed and no doubt are saying to themselves, "I don't talk to myself!" Working on Self-Esteem requires managing our self-talk. We need to talk ourselves out of the internal catastrophizing, blaming and awfulizing that we often fall victim too.

Most importantly, we need to do more than think it, talk it or read it. We need to live it! This reminds me of a favorite story. There was a salesperson who lived and breathed Self-Esteem. He had read everything about it. He listened to tapes about Self-Esteem when he woke up in the morning and he had affirmations stuck to his mirror and attached to the door of his "fridge." This person had the best Self-Esteem of anyone I ever knew. The only issue was, he never left his house.

Where we learn Self-Esteem, where we practice it is out in the world—out in messy, chaotic and never perfect life. Life comes at you every moment. It surrounds you with learning opportunities, and it rewards those who are up to the challenge, however, you gotta leave the house!

We each need to take our *unique, self-acceptance, funny and truth-telling* selves out into the real world to truly learn about ourselves and to learn to have Esteem for ourselves.

Oh, about my speech—I got over it! I'm a unique individual (I'm not my speech!). I've been through really disastrous speeches before and survived. I can accept that every once in a while, I'm going to be less than perfect. I'll have other speeches that will rival *The Poseidon Adventure!* After all, it was just a speech. It wasn't about world peace or ending world hunger. Most of all, I enjoy speaking and, the fact is, I can't quit speaking because I'm booked. (It's like the George Burns' joke, "I'm booked, I can't die.")

So, read this wonderful book, take to heart the lessons, anecdotes and affirmations. Then leave the house and learn!

Larry Wilson
Pecos River Learning Centers Inc.
Minneapolis, Minnesota

Introduction

One legacy that tells you about a man is his philosophy of life. William J. McGrane, CPAE, founder of the McGrane Self-Esteem Institute, was a master teacher. However, his personal history is filled with his own pain and unintact Self-Esteem. As a small boy, he constantly asked two questions because of what he observed: "How come I (and others) hurt so much?" and "What can be done about it?" He consciously began qualitatively researching Self-Esteem when he was a senior in high school. Dad knew there had to be an answer to what caused his internal pain.

In college, Dad studied the dictionary and learned the power of words. He became a wordsmith and gradually intimidated those around him. He *felt* powerful for a fleeting moment, and then the internal pain would increase. He continued his search to relieve the pain.

When I was a child, my dad did not have intact Self-Esteem. He was still searching for the reason he hurt inside, even though things looked great on the outside. As a result of this lack of skill, I was one of the beneficiaries of his sharp tongue. He would "slice-and-dice" me with his languaging.

In 1967, he went to a Larry Wilson program and discovered one of his missing pieces—he talked too much! He consciously started asking questions because he knew it was one way to be silent and listen. Dad began receiving better outcomes and some of his pain was released. However, something was still absent—most of the internal pain remained. He was still harming people's Self-Esteem with his powerful languaging. Dad continued his qualitative research on Self-Esteem, determined to find the answer to: "How come I (and others) hurt so much? and What can be done about it?"

In March of 1976 Dad, my brother Bob and I attended an L.S. Barksdale's *Breakthrough In Awareness Program*. It was during this program that everything came together for my father. He finally discovered his last missing piece—value judging was causing his internal pain! He described it as "the 4th of July and New Year's Eve all wrapped-up in one." It was his own personal pain that allowed him to recognize it when he saw it! All of his schooling, reading, studying, seminars, listening to audiocassette tapes and his qualitative researching of Self-Esteem finally came together. Immediately, his behavior began to change. He no longer used his wordsmith skills to "destroy" or "slice-and-dice" people. Dad went from being a "roaring lion" to a "gentle fawn." I watched this process as he refined his skills and changed his behavior. He modeled Self-Esteem behavior.

The quest my father had to know himself so he could support others was so intense, it became one of his life's passions. His philosophy of life was, "Build your Self-Esteem daily, so you can give yourself away with T.U.A. (Total Unconditional Acceptance) and then watch what happens." Each day Dad would reach out and "People Read" at least one person. His outcome was to bring at least one person into aliveness before noon.

Dad became a master model and teacher of three skills: Self-Esteem, the Art of External Listening and the Art of Asking Questions. Since he walked his talk and preached what he practiced, I was open to accepting his knowledge and skills. He was a master resource to me. Dad's greatest contribution to the world was his qualitative research on Self-Esteem—the self respect you *feel* for yourself.

It took several years to complete the loose ends of Dad's estate. This was my last chance to experience what my father's work world was like. Looking back, I encourage you to accept with honor and privilege the opportunity to conclude your family's affairs. You will learn so much about yourself and your loved ones by taking the time to appreciate their past. Whether you perceive it as pleasant or unpleasant, the process will have many lessons for your own life. It lets you live in the moment so you can prepare for your future.

Have you discovered that the process of a relationship with someone, dead or alive, is always ongoing? The last words my dad and I said to each other were, "I love you!" About eighteen months after his death someone asked me, "Are you over it?" I said, "Does one ever get over the life and death of a loved one, especially one of your greatest mentors?" My answer was based on what I now know. I *feel* complete about my relationship with Dad and what he means to me. Tomorrow, or even a moment from now, that may all change. The letter in the back of this book is an example of this change for me.

Miriam Burkart, who was my father's working associate for fifteen years, single-handedly helped bring out his unique ideas, creating what you are now about to read. Miriam has always been satisfied to be a "behind-the-scenes" person, showing her dedication by supporting and helping to develop the McGrane Self-Esteem Institute into what it is today. While William J. McGrane, CPAE was the founder, it is important to acknowledge Miriam's ongoing commitment to enhance the Self-Esteem of the world. THANK YOU MIRIAM!

A major cornerstone of William J. McGrane's life was the question, "What have you left behind to grow?" One of the legacies my father left behind was his two-minute "Brighten Your Day" recorded Self-Esteem messages. This resource of in-spiration was only a phone call away to everyone.

Now, you can read these two-minute messages. Dad's original thoughts and *feelings* will help you know and under-stand yourself and others. One of his most powerful skills was "The Art of Asking Questions." Notice how each of Dad's messages asks compelling questions that can impact your life.

Your decision to pick up this book indicates you are seek-ing insight and wisdom. Begin by taking a two-minute break every day and discover practical ways to enhance your Self-Esteem. These pages give you Dad's core criteria on "how to" integrate the Self-Esteem principles into your daily routine. "You either believe it or you don't"—he believed it and lived it!

Bill McGrane, III
President of McGrane Self-Esteem Institute

How To Use And Get The Most Out of This Book

This book is a result of William J. McGrane's "two-minute" phone messages. He wanted to give people practical ways to practice and integrate Self-Esteem behavior into their daily lives. You could read the entire book, cover-to-cover, or you may want to take a couple of minutes a day to read one message, then act on the suggestions Bill gives you.

You will notice that every message ends with the words **"and then, watch what happens!"** Bill's favorite song was *Watch What Happens.* He integrated this into each of his two-minute messages. He believed the more you notice everything around you, the more apt you are to take charge of your life and create your life the way you want it. **"And then, watch what happens"** was Bill's way of reminding you to listen, hear, see and notice how you *feel* when you practice these Self-Esteem ideas. He believed and said, "With intact Self-Esteem, happiness and success are inevitable!"

Chapter One

Self-Esteem—
The Main Ingredient!

Self-Esteem—The Main Ingredient!

Self-Esteem is a life and death issue! Only when you *feel* respectful of yourself can you be respectful of others and other living things. You can give only what you have, nothing more. Therefore, you love, earn money, communicate, have relationships, manage, teach, sell, parent, nurture and accept differences based only on your Self-Esteem!

Self-Esteem, as I use the term, is the self respect you *feel* for yourself. It is a *feeling!* Psychiatrist and author Carl Jung once said, "We need not pretend to understand the world only by intellect; we apprehend it just as much by *feeling.*" Self-Esteem is at the core of all you think, say, do and *feel.* Self-Esteem affects all seven areas of your life: Spiritual, Social, Mental, Physical, Financial, Family and Career. You can observe Self-Esteem in the behavior you and others display on a moment-to-moment basis. Please be aware that your Self-Esteem is always fluctuating, it is always in process, it is intangible and it is recognized in your behavior. As a result, you may *feel* very respectful of yourself one moment, while in the next your Self-Esteem can be in the pits.

Let us understand what Self-Esteem is not. Self-Esteem is not egotism, self-concept, self-confidence or self-image. Egotism is self-centeredness, a constant excessive reference to oneself. Self-concept is what you think about your developed and undeveloped areas (skills). Self-confidence is a belief or trust in yourself. Self-image is an imitation or representation of a person. It is not real. It is what you would "like" to present to the world.

Self-Esteem has nothing to do with how much money you have or make, your reputation, the job or career you have, your race, the clothes you wear, your religion, your educational level, your ethnic background, what you own, your sex, where you live or your zip code. It does not matter how you have focused your life. Self-Esteem is very simple—once again, it is the respect you *feel* for yourself! Carl Jung said, "Simple things are always the most difficult. In actual life, it requires the greatest discipline to be simple, and the acceptance of oneself is the essence of the problem and the epitome of a whole outlook upon life."

Many people center their lives around spiritual beliefs. The religions of the world have, at their core, beliefs such as: "All life is sacred" (Hinduism). "Gaining a complete knowledge of the inner self" (Buddhism). "Love thy neighbor as thyself" (Judaism/Christianity). In our Western Judeo-Christian culture, many of us have not been encouraged to love ourselves. This is often considered egotism and unacceptable. Yet, you first have to love yourself before you can love others. I also personally believe that Self-Esteem is at the core of moving toward your spiritual excellence. The respect you *feel* for yourself is all you can give to yourself and others. You will learn, grow, have peace of mind, be generous, manage, accept differences and responsibility, have T.U.A. (Total Unconditional Acceptance), love, sell, teach, parent and act based on your Self-Esteem—the self-respect you *feel* for yourself. Again, you cannot give what you don't have. You can only give what you have and nothing more!

Have you ever thought you had what would bring you happiness? You were satisfied, however, something was still missing. You felt unfulfilled.

Value judging is the only thing that will injure or destroy your Self-Esteem. It is comparing your values with the values of others to find their agreement or disagreement. Most value judging, about 90% of it, is done on an unconscious level; you don't even know you are doing it. However, you *feel* it! Some examples of value judging include: name calling, sarcasm, labeling, controlling, put downs, comparison, criticism and putting people on a pedestal.

You are born with intact Self-Esteem. That is your birthright! Gradually, your Self-Esteem can be diminished from you by significant others: mothers, fathers, teachers, adults and peers. You'll never reclaim it until you have *somebody* who is genuinely interested in you. They help you reclaim your Self-Esteem and make it a skill. Once you have a skill, no one can take it away from you!

When I was a boy, I lived in the small town of Sugar Notch,

Pennsylvania. From age seven to seventeen my father was on welfare. For most of my early life I *felt* like a nobody. I lived in an unintact Self-Esteem environment. My mother and father *felt* like nobodies, and my two sisters *felt* like nobodies. Then in the ninth grade, a teacher said, "Bill, I believe you can win the Latin metal." Now I never raised my hand in class, never spoke up in groups, yet here was a teacher who believed I could win the Latin metal. With her help, I did! Then as a senior in high school, a teacher said, "I believe you can win the public speaking contest." I didn't believe her. She said, "We're going to practice, rehearse and drill until you get that skill." That was the beginning of my journey of doing qualitative research to discover the answers to these questions: "How come I hurt so much?" "How come other people hurt so much?" and "What can be done about it?"

When I first started studying Self-Esteem, people ridiculed and abandoned the idea as a "throw-away concept." Now, they're two of the hottest words in the English language because everybody is going through pain. The economy, relationships, marriages, families, teenagers, baby boomers and senior citizens all give us great opportunities to see the differences between self-image and Self-Esteem. Self-Esteem is the bottom line for the future, for family and business relationships. When you live by self-image, you are guaranteed pain because you base your life on comparison and value judging. When you have Self-Esteem, which is the self-respect you *feel* for yourself, then you have "freedom." It does not matter if you are young, or old or somewhere in-between; we all have inside *feelings*. No one can know what you are *feeling* inside unless you let them know. Things may appear "perfect" on the outside while you may be "dying" on the inside.

Right now, the world's number one epidemic is self-image. Take a look at teens and how this period in life is called "the lost years." Suicides, alcoholism, drugs and babies born out of wedlock are all examples of unintact Self-Esteem. Look at families and people in a mid-life crisis, which can start anywhere between thirty-five and fifty. Eighty million baby boomers are now at that stage! How are they dealing with the transition? How about the time they invested in getting everything, wanting the biggest house, the biggest car and the biggest income? What will they do now with down sizing, merges, acquisitions and companies having other major challenges?

Feelings of Self-Esteem can only flourish in an atmosphere where:

• Individual differences are appreciated.
• Communication is open.
• Mistakes are tolerated.
• Rules are flexible.

Robert W. Darvin, founder, president and chief executive officer of Scandinavian Design, Inc. said, "There's only one thing that counts in a business: building the Self-Esteem of your employees. Nothing else matters because what they *feel* about themselves is what they give to your customers. If an employee comes to work not liking his job, not *feeling* respect for himself, you can be sure your customers will go away not liking or *feeling* good about your company."

I predict people will be focusing on values that are most important. They are going to be focusing on building their Self-Esteem and leaving their self-images behind. They will say their actions are going to be in the direction of personal freedom: taking care of myself; taking care of my family; taking care of my job; taking care of my business; valuing my employees; and most importantly, expressing all the skills I am willing to learn as a result of not comparing myself with anyone else again. They will be investing those skills in making their communities better by volunteering 10% of their time to the community. I call this "tithing" their talent. When this happens, we're going to have a unique country that will be an example, causing all the countries of the world to say, "We want to learn what you have learned to make America free."

Take action now with your Self-Esteem because:
"What the mind attends to, the mind considers.
What the mind does not consider, the mind dismisses.
What the mind continually considers, the mind believes.
And what the mind believes, the mind eventually does."
—Author Unknown

"Life Is A Series of New Beginnings!"

Quote by William J. McGrane, CPAE

Chapter Two

Self-Esteem

Have You Hugged Someone Today?

Have you ever read about David, "The Bubble Boy"? He spent all except the last 15 days of his 12 years of life in a sterile plastic bubble. His immune system did not function properly. The world loved this boy. He loved life. He was intelligent. Just before he died, he winked at his doctor.

To me, the most significant memory about David, was that it took 12 years before he was hugged or touched by his mother. Think about that for a moment. What would it be like to not have never had the human touch? How do you feel about hugging? When was the last time you were hugged? Who initiated it?

I believe everyone deserves at least four hugs a day. Do you know where to go now—this moment—to get your four hugs? Are you uncomfortable reading this message about hugging? Is it easy for you to hug members of your family? When was the last time you hugged them or they hugged you? What is the reason some people avoid hugging? Is it because they were not hugged? People can only hug based on their Self-Esteem.

Virginia Satir, a family therapist, once said, "Everyone needs 12 hugs a day." Leo Buscaglia, author and speaker, hugs everyone who wants a hug. People stand in line after he speaks to receive his hug. Charlie "Tremendous" Jones, another well-known author and speaker is also known for his hugging.

Have you heard about the mad hugger? He speaks all over the United States about hugging. He is a very popular speaker.

Have you heard about the hugging squad? It consists of women who visit older people in their homes. Six or eight women go in one car; they drive up to a home, stop, rush up to the older person and proceed to give him or her 12 hugs.

Sidney Simon, who wrote the book *Caring, Feeling and Touching*, says "We are a skin hungry nation—we are starving to be touched. We all need a caring touch, a comforting touch and a soothing touch. Touching, in a caring way, is therapeutic."

What decision will you make because you read this message? Will you set up a hugging station in your home, office, church or neighborhood? Will you ask for your four hugs today? Will you hug four people today? Remember, David—The Bubble Boy. Then do it.

Hug and then, watch what happens!

> *"I now ask for and give four*
> *hugs every day."*

Do You Love Yourself?

Does anyone ever ask you just what is Self-Esteem all about? Have you ever wondered about Self-Esteem? Have you noticed there is an increased interest in Self-Esteem? People and organizations are becoming more aware that when they add just a little more Self-Esteem, more potential and productivity are released.

Self-Esteem is the core of a person's physical, mental and spiritual well-being. Self-Esteem is the self respect you *feel* for yourself. You can instantly observe a person's Self-Esteem by the way they treat you. The entire focus of Self-Esteem is on a very difficult word for many people—that word is *love*. First, love yourself. Then, and only then, can you love anyone else. In other words, you can give only what you have and no more!

In *Modern Maturity* magazine, Caroline Bird and clinical psychologist, Howard Newberger, were talking about aging and the need for love. They believe some people get into trouble because they fail to realize that love is a developmental relationship that can get broader. For example, as people progress in their loving relationships, they can allow more kinds of relationships in their lives. They can also develop deeper relationships through the years. Love of some kind is essential as long as we draw breath. It is something that we can always be learning. Is it possible that with focus and practice, the older we get, the better we get at loving ourselves and others?

Caroline Bird says, "Love is the real thing and love is an active process. Love is the overflow of our fulfillment that we give to others, to keep them in their fulfillment. There are four steps to love.

1. Loving yourself.
2. Choosing someone to love.
3. Finding out what that person needs.
4. Doing something about it."

The most challenging part is loving yourself. I believe *there is no better way to age gracefully than to develop your Self-Esteem.* The reason people and organizations strive to learn more about Self-Esteem is so they can take quantum leaps.

There you have it. Develop your Self-Esteem daily. Then you will love yourself. This is your best guarantee of success, happiness and aging gracefully.

Take action now with your Self-Esteem **and then, watch what happens!**

> *"I now love myself totally and unconditionally."*

Have You Upgraded Your Self-Esteem Lately?

How do you *feel* about this statement: "The more you know, the more you know you don't know"? Have you read about the changes in the educational process? Teachers will be held more accountable. Students will be required to accept more responsibility and discipline. Parents will be asked to be more involved with their children to guide them to prepare for life.

There is a new renaissance and commitment to excellence in education. Is excellence worth it? Nick Carter, a friend of mine says, "Everything worthwhile in life has a procedure." There is a procedure for getting dressed, preparing a meal, eating, riding a bike, playing a game and driving a car. There is also a procedure for learning and placing a high value on excellence.

Learning the basics of reading, writing, math, listening, speaking and asking questions is important. What about the most basic skill—the skill of developing intact Self-Esteem? What would need to exist for all parents, students and teachers to be taught Self-Esteem principles and to take a Self-Esteem evaluation at the beginning and end of each school year? Do you have any idea how the achievement scores would increase? Can you picture the level of family, community, national and international harmony that could be created?

What point do I want to make? It is simply this: If we want to prepare people for taking full responsibility for their lives, *we need to help them develop their Self-Esteem.*

Take action now. How intact is your Self-Esteem? What do you know about Self-Esteem? Next, evaluate the time and money you are investing in educating yourself and your family. Check the financial and psychological rewards you are receiving. If the payoff is not there to your satisfaction, then continue studying Self-Esteem. Your relationships are based on your Self-Esteem. You earn money based on your Self-Esteem. You accept responsibility for everything your think, say, do and *feel* based on your Self-Esteem. You learn based on your Self-Esteem. *Your Self-Esteem impacts all areas of your life now and in the future.*

Refine and upgrade your Self-Esteem **and then, watch what happens!**

> *"I now upgrade my Self-Esteem daily."*

Do You Help Others *Feel* Important?

Have you noticed how many companies have reduced their names to initials? Here are some examples: International Business Machines uses IBM, National Broadcasting Company uses NBC and National Cash Register uses NCR. That concept is called ephemeralization which means "less is more." In other words, it is easier to remember IBM, NBC and NCR.

With that idea in mind, I would like to introduce you to IWTFI. This means, "I Want To *Feel* Important." Sidney Simon has researched the importance of values in our life. He said that IWTFI is something we need every day, and we each have this need inside of us. Dr. Simon also says, "Self-Esteem is the bottom line for success." I believe that Self-Esteem is the first ingredient for success and for fulfilling IWTFI.

As you watch the television news, listen to the radio and look at the latest news magazines, do you observe the behavior of people daily? As you listen to the often tense conversations about the issues of the day (like abortion and euthanasia), do you immediately identify these as being Self-Esteem issues? *Everyone wants* IWTFI. It is one ingredient that is needed to help people make the best choices daily. However, if you were criticized and put down as a child, your tendency may be to criticize yourself and others as an adult.

When I meet people each day, I observe them to see if they know about IWTFI. It takes less than two minutes to notice this. You will know a person's IWTFI by their behavior. A person with IWTFI will be open, smile, be genuinely interested in you, have a great hand shake, keep eye contact, listen and hear what you are saying and ask questions. Starting now, practice these qualities of IWTFI with everyone you meet. You will give undivided attention to others, have more in-depth conversations and may discover the *uniqueness of each person* you meet. As you use the IWTFI qualities, you will be exposing and enhancing your own IWTFI.

Give the next five people you meet some of your IWTFI. Help them to *feel* important when they are with you **and then, watch what happens!**

> **"I now treat everyone I meet with IWTFI."**

How Do You Promote Peace And Harmony?

How do you *feel* about mass murders—where one human being in pain kills and injures numerous others? Newspaper, television and radio report these kinds of things as the nation's worst slaughters. The murders all happen in a very short period of time. The person doing the killing may have been depressed, lost a job, always quiet or angry.

Can you see the damaging effects of unintact Self-Esteem? Self-Esteem is the self respect you *feel* for yourself. People who commit this kind of crime had intact Self-Esteem when they were born. Yet, during their lives someone taught them not to love themselves. Gradually, they became angry. They repeated that behavior until the pain was so intense they *felt* they could only find peace in killing. This is a perfect example of people who were devalued during their lifetimes.

What can we learn from these events? I believe we need to appreciate the importance of affirming children starting at a very early age and continue the process for a lifetime. Do you compliment children when you meet them? Do you find it easy to help people *feel* comfortable when you meet them? Do you make it a habit to avoid criticizing people? It requires diligent effort to change a habit.

Every day we add a new layer to our life. If the significant people in our lives helped us to *feel* important, then it is easy to help others *feel* important. Millions of people wake up every day lonely and depressed. Picture what would happen if they *met* someone like you who *had* intact Self-Esteem. They could receive compliments from you every day.

You can never take a vacation from your Self-Esteem because you are the only one who is with you 24 hours a day. You have choices. *First, decide to develop your Self-Esteem by being kind and gentle with yourself.* Be aware of your self-talk. Notice how you treat yourself. Do you reward yourself daily? How well do you pamper you? You have the potential to influence the Self-Esteem of others to the degree you have intact Self-Esteem. You can only give what you have, nothing more. How would you *feel* if someone would say to you, "I like me best when I am with you"?

Compliment someone daily **and then, watch what happens!**

> *"I now affirm one person every day to increase peace and harmony in the world."*

Is Your Self-Image Destroying Your Self-Esteem?

Have you noticed how often the words Self-Esteem are used in newspapers, television, radio and when people talk about education and success? Do you know the difference between self-image and Self-Esteem? Would you be interested in discovering a way for you to *feel* respect for yourself daily?

When I was a boy, I began asking myself two questions, "How come I and others hurt so much?" and "What can be done about it?" This began my qualitative research on Self-Esteem. The reason these questions emerged was because I personally had unintact Self-Esteem. I had a self-image! There is a great difference between self-image and Self-Esteem. Self-image is an imitation or representation of a person. It is what one would like to project to the world. It is comparison. Self-image means: I *imitate* someone. I *measure* myself against another person. I act *artificial* by trying to be someone I am not. I *gossip*. And I *envy* other people for what they have or do. Self-image destroys my Self-Esteem and causes internal pain.

Read the following words and notice how you *feel*. These are all self-image words: emotional abuse, mental illness, egocentricity, jealousy, gossip, fear, crime, rejection, depression, guilt, emptiness, praise, labeling, insecurity, addictions and indifference. The next time you see a dead tree think about all the people who are dead on the inside. They are numb. They are operating out of a self-image.

What is Self-Esteem? Self-Esteem is the self respect you *feel* for yourself. It is a *feeling*. People with intact Self-Esteem encourage others; they are sensitive to people; they give people their time and undivided attention; they have high energy; they establish mutually beneficial empathic relationships; and they are highly motivated.

The following words reflect intact Self-Esteem: peace of mind, encouragement, fulfillment, affirming, to have fun daily, patience, trust, joy, health, purpose, integrity, acceptance, creativity, forgiveness, inner-directed, commitment and responsibility. The next time you see a beautiful tree in full bloom, ask yourself, "Do I have self respect and self love?" With intact Self-Esteem, happiness and success are inevitable.

You can live a life of self-image or Self-Esteem. You have a choice. Be respectful of yourself in every behavior you choose. Reach out to others with intact Self-Esteem. Serve them in any way you can.

Choose Self-Esteem **and then, watch what happens!**

"I now choose intact Self-Esteem daily."

What's In A Name?

Do you like your name? Did your parents give you a name of someone they respected? Did your parents choose your name because of some historical or famous person? Did your parents choose your name because of some religious or biblical reference? Did your parents choose your name because they loved it?

Our name is very important to us. My name is William. My father's name was William and we named our first son William. When I was a little boy, my mother called me Billy. I did not like that name. Then I was called Bill. I accepted that name and now most people call me Bill. Few people call me William. Bill, for me, is a comfortable name.

Are you wondering how come I am focusing my attention on the importance of our names? Here is the reason. Once our family went on its annual three day outing to an Ohio State Park. While there, I stopped at the gift shop. As I was browsing, I asked the person behind the counter for her name. She said, "My name is Noreen." I said, "Do you like your name?" She said, "No, it is ugly!" I asked, "Who gave you your name?" She responded, "My mother." I asked, "Did she ever tell you how come she called you Noreen?" She commented, "Yes, it was the name of someone she loved very much. My mother said, 'If I ever have a little girl, I will name her Noreen.'" I said, "So, of all the names your mother could have chosen, she gave you a name she loved." Noreen said, "I never thought of it that way. To think it took me this long to appreciate the importance of my name. Noreen is a beautiful name." Then she thanked me.

What do you know about your name? Have you ever inquired about the specifics of exactly how your name was chosen? Do you know the meaning of your name? For example, William is old high German—Will helmet. It means: will, desire, resolute, protector. Have fun with your name. Discover its origins. Interview your family members who know the reasons you received your name. There is a story behind your name—discover it, write it down or put it on audiotape. Enjoy your name!

When you meet a person, ask for their name. Listen for the correct pronunciation. Use their name five times before you end your conversation **and then, watch what happens!**

> *"I now value my name and the name
> of every person I meet."*

Do You Use Affirmations?

Do you say affirmations every day? Do you write affirmations every day? Do you affirm other people daily?

Conrad Baars in his book, *Born Only Once* says, "Affirmation is a state of *being*. Affirmation is first of all *affectivity*—a matter of *feeling*. Only secondarily is it *effectivity*—a matter of *doing*." Thomas A. Kane in his book, *The Healing Touch of Affirmation* says, "Affirmation comes from the word *affirmare* and means to make firm, to give strength, to make strong. It implies assent, agreement, consent, a willingness to say 'Yes' to all creation." Affirmation is T.U.A. (Total Unconditional Acceptance) of yourself and your potential. It is also T.U.A. of others and their potential.

The effectivity, or *doing* part of an affirmation, is a statement or declaration which encourages you to be who you are so that your potential may *BE* developed and realized. These affirmations work only when you combine thinking, plus *feelings* and follow-up with action. Read these affirmations, then design your own and say them several times a day.

1. I welcome the new day.
2. I have wonderful expectations of this day.
3. I *feel* free to move on to healthier ideas, thoughts and emotions.
4. Today, I take steps toward attaining my outcomes.
5. Today, I listen attentively to all those I encounter.
6. Today, I am aware of my own *feelings* and affirm my self respect.
7. I now make decisions competently.
8. I meet new opportunities with courage.
9. I use words which emanate power.
10. I create my own happiness.
11. I am a resourceful person.
12. I see the many things I can learn from others.
13. I can make my dreams become reality.
14. I possess the courage to choose the direction of my life.
15. I value each moment.
16. I take charge of my life today.
17. I am appreciated and I appreciate others.
18. I give to others unconditionally.
19. I am tactful with others.
20. I accept my mistakes and let them contribute to my learning and development.

21. I am healthy.
22. Today, I let go of the things I cannot control.
23. I make wise choices every day.
24. I am motivated to pursue my outcomes.
25. I have intact Self-Esteem.

Decide now to design and say your affirmations daily **and then, watch what happens!**

> *"I now invest in writing and saying affirmations daily."*

Are You Responsible For Your Life?

Are you a student of current events? Do you like to know what is happening in the world? Or are you only interested in certain issues that influence your life? As you tune in the world daily, do you sometimes want to avoid learning about other people's challenges? Are you willing to accept the responsibility of helping at least one person with their Self-Esteem every day? Are you committed to help make the world a place where people have Total Unconditional Acceptance (T.U.A.) of themselves and each other?

Taking responsibility puts you in charge. You are no longer behaving like a victim. You depend on yourself for your well-being. You know you don't have to live up to anyone else's expectations. Responsibility involves internal and external self-control. When people understand they are responsible for themselves, they realize their behavior is a major influence on what happens to them. They learn they are not at the mercy of others. Nor can they blame or hold others responsible for their outcomes.

Please repeat these statements.
1. I now accept responsibility for my own life.
2. I am the master of my present and future.
3. I determine my own outcomes and my own lifestyle.

Repeating affirmations like those is how responsibility manifests itself in self-talk. Individuals with unintact Self-Esteem problems either habitually fail to accept responsibility for themselves or habitually take too much responsibility.

Each person needs to accept responsibility for themselves. With intact Self-Esteem, it is easier to accept responsibility for everything we think, say, do and *feel*. These choices lead to a balanced lifestyle.

Picture what would happen in a world where everyone accepted responsibility, with integrity, for everything they thought, said, did and *felt*. Happiness, peace, harmony and cooperation would be the outcomes. Accepting responsibility with integrity is the best test of intact Self-Esteem.

Evaluate how you are accepting responsibility with integrity in all areas of your life: Spiritual, Mental, Financial, Social, Physical, Family and Career **and then, watch what happens!**

> *"I now accept responsibility*
> *for my own life."*

What Is Your Declaration of Self-Esteem?

Do you ever wonder how the Self-Esteem ideas are applied in real life? One of our graduates, who is a teacher, encourages her students every school day to read *My Declaration of Self-Esteem* written by Virginia Satir. She asked the students to write about what the Self-Esteem declaration meant to them. Please read some of their comments below. As you read, picture what could happen if all children affirmed their Self-Esteem daily.

1. "The *Declaration of Self-Esteem* means to me that no one else in the whole world is like me. It makes me *feel* happy inside to know that I'm the only me. No other person thinks like me, talks like me or does different things like me."

2. "*My Declaration of Self-Esteem* means I am me. I think it means I have my own *feelings*. I can see, hear, *feel*,

think, say and do. I am my own special person. I can discard behavior which is unfitting. That means if I have a pimple on my nose, I do not have to keep it there. I can discard it. Because I care for myself, I can work a little harder at washing my face. I own myself."

3. *"I AM ME.'* The first part of the declaration it is telling the truth. It tells me that there is no one exactly like me. I think people don't think about what they are saying when they say this affirmation. I try to think about what I am saying."

4. *"I AM ME.'* I think it means that I am free. I am responsible for my actions and words. If I hurt someone's *feelings*, I am hurting myself. Only I control my actions. There is nobody else like me. Some people may like the same things as I do; however, they are not the same as me. I am me and I am OK."

How do you *feel* about these four 10-year-olds and what they are learning about Self-Esteem? Read Virginia Satir's, *My Declaration of Self-Esteem* on the next page, and decide how you *feel* **and then watch what happens!**

> **"I now read my declaration of
> Self-Esteem daily."**

MY DECLARATION OF SELF-ESTEEM

I AM ME

IN ALL THE WORLD, THERE IS NO ONE ELSE EXACTLY LIKE ME

EVERYTHING THAT COMES OUT OF ME IS AUTHENTICALLY MINE

BECAUSE I ALONE CHOSE IT — I OWN EVERYTHING ABOUT ME

MY BODY, MY FEELINGS, MY MOUTH, MY VOICE, ALL MY ACTIONS,

WHETHER THEY BE TO OTHERS OR TO MYSELF — I OWN MY FANTASIES,

MY DREAMS, MY HOPES, MY FEARS — I OWN ALL MY TRIUMPHS AND

SUCCESSES, ALL MY FAILURES AND MISTAKES   BECAUSE I OWN ALL OF

ME, I CAN BECOME INTIMATELY ACQUAINTED WITH ME — BY SO DOING

I CAN LOVE ME AND BE FRIENDLY WITH ME IN ALL MY PARTS — I KNOW

THERE ARE ASPECTS ABOUT MYSELF THAT PUZZLE ME, AND OTHER

ASPECTS THAT I DO NOT  KNOW — BUT AS LONG AS I AM

FRIENDLY AND LOVING TO MYSELF, I CAN COURAGEOUSLY

AND HOPEFULLY LOOK FOR SOLUTIONS TO THE PUZZLES

AND FOR WAYS TO FIND OUT MORE ABOUT ME — HOWEVER I

LOOK AND SOUND, WHATEVER I SAY AND DO, AND WHATEVER

I THINK AND FEEL AT A GIVEN MOMENT IN TIME IS AUTHENTICALLY

ME — IF LATER SOME PARTS OF HOW I LOOKED, SOUNDED, THOUGHT

AND FELT TURN OUT TO BE UNFITTING, I CAN DISCARD THAT WHICH IS

UNFITTING, KEEP THE REST, AND INVENT SOMETHING NEW FOR THAT

WHICH I DISCARDED — I CAN SEE, HEAR, FEEL, THINK, SAY, AND DO

I HAVE THE TOOLS TO SURVIVE, TO BE CLOSE TO OTHERS, TO BE PRO-

DUCTIVE, AND TO MAKE SENSE AND ORDER OUT OF THE WORLD OF

PEOPLE AND THINGS OUTSIDE OF ME — I OWN ME, AND THEREFORE

I CAN ENGINEER ME — I AM ME AND

I AM OKAY

Virginia Satir

Do You Evaluate Your Behavior?

Would you like to play a Self-Esteem "true or false" game? Write your answers of "true" or "false" on a piece of paper. Here we go.

1. I had intact Self-Esteem when I was born.
2. My present Self-Esteem was created by significant others in my life.
3. My present attitudes are affirming or unaffirming, based on the role models in my life.
4. The definition of Self-Esteem is the way I *feel* about myself.
5. My ability to describe my *feelings* helps me to reduce tension and distress.
6. My ability to listen to others is an indication of my Self-Esteem.
7. Finality Statements kill Self-Esteem communication.
8. Finishing sentences for others is unintact Self-Esteem behavior.
9. Interrupting others is a sign of unintact Self-Esteem.
10. Criticizing others shows unintact Self-Esteem.
11. Putting people down is an unintact Self-Esteem choice.
12. Name calling demonstrates unintact Self-Esteem.
13. Labeling other people is unintact Self-Esteem behavior.
14. Comparing yourself with others harms your Self-Esteem.
15. Trying to prove yourself to other people is a sign of unintact Self-Esteem.
16. Avoiding responsibility for everything you think, say, do or *feel* is unintact Self-Esteem behavior.
17. Getting drunk is unintact Self-Esteem behavior.
18. Dependency on drugs is a sign of unintact Self-Esteem.
19. Depending on others for you to *feel* good is unintact Self-Esteem behavior.
20. Choosing to be healthy is an intact Self-Esteem choice.
21. Choosing to be sick is an unintact Self-Esteem choice.
22. Shyness is a sign of unintact Self-Esteem.

23. Depressing *feelings* is a sign of unintact Self-Esteem.
24. Enthusiasm and a zest for life is intact Self-Esteem behavior.
25. Overeating is unintact Self-Esteem behavior.
26. Obesity and being overweight is unintact Self-Esteem behavior.
27. Procrastination shows unintact Self-Esteem.
28. Inability to make decisions is unintact Self-Esteem behavior.
29. Building and maintaining relationships is a sign of intact Self-Esteem.
30. Releasing your full potential is intact Self-Esteem behavior.
31. Holding grudges is unintact Self-Esteem behavior.
32. Fear of speaking in groups is a sign of unintact Self-Esteem.
33. Career unhappiness reflects unintact Self-Esteem.
34. Complimenting people is intact Self-Esteem behaior.
35. Creating an affirming lifestyle is intact Self-Esteem behavior.
36. Giving recognition to others is intact Self-Esteem behavior.

If you said "true" to each of these statements, you deserve 100%. And this is what you deserve with your Self-Esteem every day.

Review your behavior daily to discover if it helps create intact Self-Esteem in yourself and others **and then, watch what happens!**

> *"I now evaluate my behavior and Self-Esteem daily."*

What Are Your Values?

How do you *feel* about the conflict that exists in the world? If you look at it, you will recognize that conflict results from opposing values. Everyone has a set of values. These are intense beliefs about specific ideas, people or situations. For example, if I say, "All violence is a request for love"—there could be some people with a different point of view who may not agree.

Do you recall the nuclear reactor meltdown that occurred many years ago in Russia? The Russians kept this information secret. This is an example of values conflict. Over 3,000 people in Sweden had consequences because of radioactive fallout.

The value of life is an important issue for many people. Every day you make values choices that trigger pain or pleasure. The people you associate with is a values choice. The person you marry is a values choice. The work you do is a values choice. Where you live is a values choice. The causes you work for a values choice. How we treat others is a values choice. Our behavior tells the world our values.

There are universal values such as peace, honesty and integrity. Two ultimate values are wisdom and love. Our values are set early in childhood. Research shows that by age 10 we have well-defined values. After age 10 we are bombarded with invitations to change our values. Television, magazines, newspapers and other people may influence our values. So our values are subject to change.

There are four value systems. First, some people are in the *Challenger* values system. They are very self-centered. Next, others are in the *In-Betweener* values system. These people have difficulty making decisions. Third, still others are in the *Traditional* values system which is based on a system of principles. Finally, some people are in the *Synthesis* values system. These people can get along with anyone. They are clear. They are leaders. They have integrity. Only two percent of the population are in the Synthesis Value System. It takes intact Self-Esteem to reach the Synthesis Values System.

When our values are clear, decision making is easy. Values

clarification is a lifelong process. Only your Self-Esteem can create clarity.

Observe the ongoing scenario of your life, make your own values decision **and then, watch what happens!**

> *"I now clarify my values to find peace and fulfillment in my personal and professional life."*

Do You Accept Responsibility For Your Part In the World?

How do you *feel* about all of the terrorism in the world? The words "terror" and "hostage" are commonplace today. When a person or a country has intact Self-Esteem, there isn't any terrorism or hostages.

I am committed to Global Self-Esteem. I want to influence every country, state, city, home and individual. The ideal outcome is for everyone to have intact Self-Esteem. When this occurs, everyone will accept responsibility for everything he or she thinks, says, does and *feels*.

Can you picture what a city with intact Self-Esteem would look like? There would be no crime, no violence, full employment, well educated children and adults, people committed to serve others, and it would be the model city of the world. Is it possible? I believe it is! All we have to do is decide to be responsible and then act on that decision.

Webster's Dictionary defines responsibility as "answerable, accountable, reliable, trustworthy and dependable." William Glasser, a psychologist and author of *Control Theory*, defines responsibility as "the ability to fulfill our own needs and to do so in a way that does not deprive others of the ability to fulfill their needs."

When people's Self-Esteem is squashed, there can be terrorism and war. The greatest gift you can give yourself is to be responsible. Blame, guilt, shame, hate, remorse and resentment are ways of escaping responsibility. Only your Self-Esteem will cause you to accept responsibility for everything you think, say, do and *feel.*

How are you responsible? You are responsible when you:
1. Perform tasks without being told every time.
2. Know the outcomes you want to obtain.
3. Do not blame anyone for anything.
4. Make agreements and commitments and keep them.
5. Take charge of your life.
6. Build your Self-Esteem daily.

So celebrate your Self-Esteem daily. Create a Self-Esteem environment wherever you are **and then, watch what happens!**

> *"I now celebrate my Self-Esteem by accepting responsibility for everything I think, say, do and feel."*

Do You Describe Your *Feelings*?

Do you listen to the way people speak? Do you listen to them say "I think" and "I *feel*"? Is it easier for people to say what they think or say what they *feel*? Is it easy for people to describe their *feelings*?

Recall a time when you *felt* excited. Can you describe the experience in great detail? Can you describe your *feelings* about the event? A professional speaker, Bobbie Sims, sent me a copy of her book called, *Making A Difference In Your World.* There is a section on *feelings.* She says the door to the human heart can be opened only from the inside. It is a personal choice. *Feelings* are always the result of a person's perception and interpretation .

John Powell, author of *Unconditional Love,* writes about *feelings.* He said, "During my childhood and youth, the role models in my life were busy surviving a depression and then a war. In that environment, *feelings* seemed like weaknesses." He frequently heard such remarks as, "You've got your *feelings* on your sleeve. *Feelings* are a weakness. Be BIG! Be strong! You 'should' not *feel* that way." John Powell's interpretation of those messages was, "Maybe I 'shouldn't' *feel* what I *feel*, and if I do, I 'must' never let my *feelings* show." He says changing that conclusion and learning to value and experience his *feelings* has required much work and rethinking on his part.

I believe feelings are core to our existence. For example, picture that you are awakened in the middle of the night by a very loud noise. Your feelings are *pure* and immediate, usually intense and very short-term. You may feel fear accompanied with fight or flight. When you determine the source of the noise, and discover that it is not a threat, your fear dissipates. Now, you have a choice of how you will feel.

William Glasser in his book, *Take Effective Control of Your Life*, notes: "Short-term *pure* feelings begin to attenuate (weaken) as soon as they occur. They are completely superseded in a very short time by behavior you choose. What to do, think, and feel—you choose, however you do not choose the *pure* feelings that precede any of these behaviors: Those are built into your control systems. It is from these simple *pure* feelings, which are tied to your survival, that all of your complex feelings eventually evolve and become a vital component of your behavior."

Feelings add extra dimension and richness to life. Give yourself permission to feel your *pure* feelings—you do not have to act on them. Next pause, breathe, repeat the affirmation—"I am calm and relaxed." Then choose the behavior that will give you the best outcome. This will help you describe *feelings*.

Decide now to educate your *feelings* **and then, watch what happens!**

> **"*I now know how to describe my feelings.*"**

Is Your Lifestyle Full Of High Energy?

Are you a high energy person? Are you a low energy person? Are you drained at the end of the day? Do you go to work tired? Do you need coffee to increase your energy? Do you need cigarettes , alcohol or drugs to "give you a lift"? Are you part of the human energy crisis or are you a naturally high energy person?

I once went into a store and watched the energy level of the employees. The store was air conditioned, and the owner invested much money in equipment and atmosphere. There was one missing ingredient. The employees had low energy for life, for the customers, for the company and for themselves. These employees took energy away from people. They created a toxic environment.

As you perform your job, what takes away your energy and what increases your energy? For example, when you speak, do people listen? Listening creates energy. Ignoring someone takes away energy. Asking questions creates energy. Making statements can take energy away. Giving people affirming Self-Esteem messages creates energy. Criticizing, blaming or punishing kills energy. Giving recognition creates energy. Withholding recognition kills energy. Asking someone for help creates energy. Denying your *feelings* takes away energy.

Would you like to have high energy every day? If you said "yes," then consider doing some of the following.

1. Release criticizing yourself and others.
2. Release comparing yourself with others.
3. Release getting angry and resentful.
4. Release blaming anyone for anything.
5. Release working or living in a toxic environment.
6. Start giving Self-Esteem messages to everyone.
7. Start giving compliments to everyone.
8. Start an exercise program and learn to relax.
9. Start a nutritional eating program.
10. Start learning new skills daily.

Hang around high energy people **and then, watch what happens!**

> *"I now know that an intact Self-Esteem lifestyle creates high energy."*

Do You Ask Questions?

When people ask you questions, are you comfortable or uncomfortable? What kind of questions help you to *feel* at ease? Are they safe questions like: "What is your name?" "Where do you live?" "Where do you work?" Are you relaxed when you answer those questions?

What about questions from doctors, lawyers, bankers, teachers, dentists, friends, spouses and children? Have you experienced times as a child when you asked questions and were told, "You ask too many questions"?

Is it possible you still hear those voices, and this causes you to be afraid to ask questions? Are you unlikely to ask for directions? Have you ever needed to ask someone to repeat information, yet chose not to ask? Are you ever concerned about asking for your missing piece (that which is absent from your life, be it a need, want or value)?

Were you ever put down for asking a question in school? Have you ever been uncomfortable asking a question at work? Did you ever *feel* rejected for asking questions? Has anyone ever criticized you for asking questions? What does it *feel* like when these things happen? I once talked to a woman who said, "I tremble when I need to ask questions." She was afraid of rejection and ridicule.

When you go for a job interview, what is the number one skill of the interviewer? Is it "asking questions"? Is his outcome to learn as much about you as possible to determine if you are the best choice for the organization? What if you are asked surprise questions like, "What do you like least about yourself?" or "What do you like best about yourself?" Are you prepared to be relaxed, calm and in charge when being interviewed?

When you socialize with people, do you ask questions to improve your conversation skills? Would you like to earn more money? Are you interested in improving your relationships? Is it important that you upgrade your communication competence?

If you answered "yes" to any of these questions, then may I suggest you learn the Art of Asking Questions **and then, watch what happens!**

> *"I now decide to improve my personal power by learning the Art of Asking Questions."*

The Test of Greatness: What Have You Left Behind To Grow?

A mentor is a resource person who accepts you totally and unconditionally, never devalues you through criticism, never tells you what to do, never gives you answers, or uses guilt, blame or punishment. This person(s) asks questions and listens and helps you discover answers for yourself. He or she can give you direction and help you make excellent choices.

When half of the world is a mentor to the other half, world peace and tranquillity will be the outcome. Individuals will then take a quantum leap to strive for excellence in order to make a significant contribution. They will increase their productivity to model behavior and create a climate where each person can thrive.

A mentor:
1. Is an example of excellence.
2. Has a thirst to learn.
3. Is open to all experiences.
4. Avoids comparison with others.
5. Knows what he or she is looking for and knows it when he or she sees it.

6. Is spontaneous and childlike vs. childish.
7. Comes from abundance vs. scarcity, to share all knowledge.
8. Is congruent.
9. Passionately commits to 100% ownership of his or her personal power.
10. Encourages all persons who are influenced by him or her to retain 100% ownership of their personal power.
11. Accepts responsibility for everything he or she thinks, says, does and *feels*.
12. Has the capacity to mentally experience an outcome in advance of reality.
13. Has the vision to see the big picture of his or her life.
14. Enjoys a balanced lifestyle: Spiritual, Mental, Financial, Social, Physical, Family and Career.
15. Generates a "WOW!" enthusiastic attitude toward living regardless of world conditions.
16. Is sensitive to all human beings.
17. Is an excellent external listener.
18. Knows how to be present to the moment and each person in the moment.
19. Knows and practices the Art of Asking Questions.
20. Gives the mentee T.U.A. and freedom to describe his message through pacing, leading and double looping.
21. Knows when to let go; avoids all dependency, guilt and blame.
22. Appreciates that the relationship may experience gradual changes including: resentment, detachment, indifference and lack of appreciation.
23. Has decided that "five-sensing life" (experiencing life with all your senses) is part of the pathway to total fulfillment.
24. Realizes that value judging is the only way to "hurt."

VALUE JUDGMENTS

I dreamt death came the other night
And heaven's gate swung wide,
An angel with halo bright
Ushered me inside.

And there! To my astonishment
Stood folks I'd judged and labeled,
As "quite unfit" of "little worth"
And "spiritually disabled."

Indignant words rose to my lips,
Yet never were set free.
For every face showed stunned surprise,
Not one expected ME!

—Author Unknown

25. Demonstrates that daily expansion of competence, reprogramming and daily action can lead the mentee to create a demand for his or her talents and skills.
26. Believes that life is a series of new beginnings and that being an unconscious incompetent can lead to being a conscious incompetent, then to being a conscious competent and gradually to being an unconscious competent where excellence becomes reflex.
27. Has the Self-Esteem to constantly look for new awareness to pursue knowledge. This will ideally lead to a significant emotional moment when the mentor can welcome the mentee to a professional level. Then both can go their separate ways to guide others to "give themselves away."
28. Builds trust and cooperation.
29. Ignores gossip, criticism and put-downs of self and others.
30. Accepts the responsibility to have the "and then some attitude," to give more.
31. Invests daily to become a superlative communicator.
32. Tithes his or her talent in the community.
33. Is aware that "the tragedy of our age is that most people die with their music still in them."
34. Knows that as a "change agent," he or she can encourage all people to feel free to describe who they are, thus generating more intimate bonds among all individuals.
35. Has intact Self-Esteem.

THE MIND
What the mind attends to, the mind considers.
What the mind does not consider, the mind dismisses.
What the mind continually considers, the mind believes.
What the mind believes, the mind eventually does.

—Author Unknown

Become a mentor **and then, watch what happens!**

"I now mentor one person a day."

Is Gossip A Self-Esteem Issue?

Do you gossip? Do you know anyone who gossips? Have you participated with others who gossip? Does your spouse gossip? Do your children gossip?

There are at least 2,700 magazines published. The next time you go to a supermarket or bookstore, notice how many headlines are all gossip. They attempt to persuade you to scan and buy the magazine to dig deeper into more gossip.

What is the purpose of gossip? My conviction is that if you gossip, you put someone "down" in an attempt to put yourself "up." With gossip, you are attempting, consciously or unconsciously, to make yourself look and *feel* better at the expense of others. You may temporarily *feel* better. Yet, in the long run you will discover that gossip is a form of comparison which damages your Self-Esteem.

In the past, many of us learned about the behavior of Pete Rose, Donald Trump, Roseanne Barr, Charles Keating and thousands of others who were in the gossip spotlight. These people became the topic of conversation for hours, days and months. Family and friends may have become involved in recounting the "scoop" to determine who had the best data and the most recent news.

When I was growing up in a small Pennsylvania town, I listened to and participated in gossip. Many ethnic groups created the climate for gossip. They would speak Italian, Polish, Slovak and Lithuanian. My parents would gossip about anyone. They had unintact Self-Esteem and attempted to pass on their "put down" comments to their children. My parents did not know that I had relationships with many of the people who belonged in those diverse groups. Therefore, I refused to gossip about them.

If you participate in consistent gossip, it intensifies your pain and influences your relationships. You are likely to associate with like-minded people who love to gossip and eventually you become the focus of gossip. People remember your conversations and gradually avoid you because you welcome every opportunity to share the latest rumors or character assassination information with anyone who will listen. Your Self-Esteem is gradually and continually destroyed.

Someone said recently that the 80's were the years of greed and the focus of the 90's is envy. Is it possible that one of the components of gossip is envy?

Webster defines *gossip* as—"to indulge in idle talk or rumors about others." Webster says *envy* is—"the painful or resentful awareness of an advantage enjoyed by another joined with a desire to possess the same advantage."

Are the 90's the Age of Envy and Gossip? Many of the 75 million Baby Boomers (those born between 1946–1964) attempted to "have it all." Now they are moving into mid-life, a phase when limits begin to surface. Millions want the fast track to success. They changed jobs and careers in an attempt to get ahead faster. Many frequently moved to more expensive homes as real estate values increased. Now, some Baby Boomers realize that they may need to buy a less expensive home because the real estate and job markets have changed. They may also realize that they have not achieved the outcomes they wanted.

Fierce competition in the workplace and a shaky corporate environment has destroyed job security. There are fewer opportunities for new positions, promotions and perks (extra benefits like bonuses, etc.). What if the economic slowdown continues during the next 10 to 20 years? Will these conditions create a fertile ground for increased gossip and envy?

The stock market crash of 1987 could have been the first bitter downturn. As we move toward the year 2000, many relationships, financial outcomes and career aspirations will be affected. How will this impact everyone's Self-Esteem?

The magazine *Psychology Today* said, "Not everyone who expected to own a home or reach other financial aims will realize them." I say, not everyone who expected to attend undergraduate, graduate or professional school will be able to afford it. Not everyone who expected to reach career objectives set in earlier, less competitive times, will succeed. Not everyone who expected to marry will find a mate. Not everyone who expected to be a parent and deferred child-bearing will be able to have a family. Not everyone who simply expected companionship will find someone to be their companion.

These realities can create the environment for more envy and gossip. As disappointment grows and as ambitions and desires are thwarted, social conditions are ripe for a destructive epidemic of envy and gossip.

So how is Self-Esteem related to gossip? Our definition of Self-Esteem is "The self respect I *feel* for myself." My self respect is demonstrated in every word and action I choose when I interact with anyone. Therefore, the person who receives the most punishment if I gossip is me. I carry those *feelings* around with me for the rest of my life. When I choose to release gossip and criticism, my *feelings* change immediately. My Self-Esteem is more intact; therefore, I respect and accept myself more.

Start now to monitor your conversations. Notice how many times gossip becomes the focus of a discussion. Then pay attention to your *feelings* afterwards. Are they painful *feelings*? This is unintact Self-Esteem.

The next time you hear someone gossip, you may want to consider saying, "Mary (use gossiper's first name), I don't know anything about that, you may want to talk with John (the center of the gossip) about it." Say that every time and then watch what happens. Your Self-Esteem will increase and you will participate in more exciting, purposeful conversations.

When you make affirming statements about people, you also create *feelings* of intact Self-Esteem for yourself. I believe our Self-Esteem determines the choices we make as we communicate with each other. There are six levels of communications.

1. Trivia
2. People talking (can be gossip with unintact Self-Esteem)
3. Opinions
4. Ideas
5. *Feelings*
6. Plateau communication

Decide now to make only affirming statements about others. It may help you be a more fulfilled human being. I believe you will be healthier. I also believe you could then have more in-depth, mutually beneficial, meaningful relationships. I *feel* you may also enjoy more peace of mind, eliminate scarcity from your life and experience more abundance.

To better ensure freedom from gossip and envy, repeat and take action on these affirmations three times a day:

1. I now accept myself totally and unconditionally.
2. I now free myself from all self-destructive criticism.
3. I now give unconditional warm regard to all people at all times.
4. I now show that I am 100% alive by acting with great enthusiasm.
5. I now choose to be completely self-determined, and I allow others that same right.
6. I now release all comparison of myself and others.

Notice and release gossip from your conversations **and then, watch what happens!**

"I now release gossip from my life."

Are Self-Image And Self-Esteem Different?

My qualitative research convinces me that Self-Esteem is the number one issue to be addressed in order to obtain the best results in life. For over 45 years, I have asked these questions.
1. How come I hurt so much?
2. How come other people hurt so much?
3. How come there are millions of people addicted to food, alcohol and drugs?
4. How come there is so much violence?
5. How come 85% of American workers are unfulfilled in what they do?

Do you remember how you *felt* about yourself 5, 10, 15 years ago? Where is your Self-Esteem now? How would you have answered the questions below 5, 10, 15 years ago and now? How will you answer them 5, 10, 15 years from now?
1. What is your purpose for living?
2. What do you like least about yourself?
3. What do you like best about yourself?
4. Who made the greatest impact on your life?
5. What did that person do for you?
6. What makes you most alive?
7. What new skill(s) will you learn in the next 5, 10, 15 years?
8. What legacy will you leave behind for having lived your life?

What memories do you want to create, to look back on 5, 10, 15 years from now, that will be different from your past memories? The reality is that you will create memories of self-image or Self-Esteem. What is the difference?

Self-image is an imitation or representation of what you want to present to the world. It is comparison of yourself and others. It is a facade, unreal.

Self-Esteem is the self respect you *feel* for yourself. How do you know if your Self-Esteem is intact? When you were born, you had intact Self-Esteem. It is your birthright. Every baby receives that gift. As soon as you met significant others, such as mother, father, other caretakers, siblings, uncles, aunts and grandparents, there were opportunities for comparison with other people's skills, appearance and behavior.

You may have heard:

1. "You are bad."
2. "You can't do that."
3. "I wish you were never born!"
4. "Why aren't you like your brother or sister?"
5. "I'm ashamed of you."
6. "You will never amount to anything."
7. "You don't live up to my expectations."
8. "Who do you think you are?"
9. "You are stupid."
10. "When will you ever learn?"

All of those words could cut you to the bone. If you heard these statements, it is likely you have remembered them all of your life. If these comments were made by your parents, they had even more destructive impact. These comments are all based on self-image, and they can destroy your Self-Esteem!

As you move forward in your life, different times of the year will cause memories to emerge. The pleasure or pain of previous experiences influences the actions you will take. For example, you may be one of many people who, during the Christmas season, do not want to go home because your parents still treat you like a child, bringing up painful childhood memories. You may make other plans to avoid such pain. Then, *feelings* of guilt could emerge. As a result, you may *feel* so pressured that you go home even though you do not want to. How do you release the painful memories and create pleasure?

Do you recall a favorite story when you were a child? Did you ask a parent to read you the story over and over again? Do you know how come you wanted to listen? Would you agree the answer is that you knew the endings which made you *feel* safe, secure and familiar? Do you still want to know the endings to *feel* safe, secure and familiar?

I believe any memory that makes you *feel* uncomfortable is something you may want to avoid; like going home for the holidays. However, what can you do to create happy memories? How can you avoid comparing NOW with then?

Accept yourself where you are right now! Avoid comparison (self-image) and create more pleasure in your life. Decide now to develop your Self-Esteem. As you *feel* better about yourself, you attract the same *feelings* from others. Begin by practicing what is written below.

1. Avoid all put downs and criticism of self and others.
2. Release all gossip.
3. Avoid hanging onto painful past experiences. Let them go.
4. Focus on the best qualities of yourself and every member of your family.
5. Be other-centered. Give your undivided attention to each person you meet.
6. Upgrade your external listening skills.
7. Refine your Art of Asking Questions.
8. Ask people to share information with you about their life experiences.
9. Develop more friendly relationships with each person in your family.
10. Create new memories so next year you can build on this year's memory investment.
11. Realize the meaning of your communication is the outcome you receive.
12. Learn the power of affirmations and affirm each person you meet.
13. Choose each word carefully. Harsh words usually cause pain and soft words usually create pleasure.

Decide to develop your Self-Esteem—the self-respect you *feel* for yourself **and then, watch what happens!**

> *"I now release self-image and*
> *develop my Self-Esteem."*

The Tree
...of Self-Image...of Self-Esteem.

(Self-Hatred)   **(Self-Respect)**

Self-Hatred	Self-Respect
• Emotional Abuse	Peace of Mind •
• Mental Illness	Encouragement •
• Egocentricity	Fulfillment •
• Dependency	Affirming •
• Jealousy	Neoteny •
• Gossip	Patience •
• Fear	Trust •
• Crime	Joy •
• Rejection	Health •
• Depression	Purpose •
• Guilt	Integrity •
• Emptiness	Acceptance •
• Praise	Creativity •
• Labeling	Forgiveness •
• Insecurity	Inner Directed •
• Addictions	Commitment •
• Indifference	Responsibility •

Value Judging & Comparison   **Love & T.U.A.**

Chapter Three

Education

Is Student Environment Important?

How do you *feel* about the information age? We started out as an agricultural society. Then we moved into the industrial age. Now we are in the information age. Our society is overwhelmed with information from radio, newspapers, magazines, TV and computers which are constantly bombarding us with data.

In spite of all of the knowledge available, our educational system is in crisis because young people are not being prepared for life. The basic skills of survival are reading, writing, math, speaking and listening. Have you observed some young people lately? My observation is that most young people are thirsty for learning. Let me give you an example.

I once gave a Self-Esteem speech to a group of vocational students. Before I spoke, there was a student meeting. Some of the students were talking and some were indifferent. Some teachers were writing and doing other work, and one teacher had his head down. Meanwhile, the meeting continued. Not one faculty member was sensitive to what was happening. No one helped to silence the group and give the elected student his or her undivided attention.

When I was introduced, I asked the student body president about the behavior of his fellow students. He said, "They were talking and were indifferent to the activities." Then I asked students to define "success." One said, "Rich." Another said, "Fulfillment." I then asked, "How many of you have a guaranteed job upon graduation?" Only a handful indicated they would go to work immediately.

The point is this, the first ingredient to meaningful relationships and career success is to build a young person's Self-Esteem. You, as a taxpayer, deserve well prepared, skilled students who take charge of their lives. Parents, students and faculty need to be accountable for creating an intact Self-Esteem environment where we, as a society, can thrive during the information age. We all need to model the behavior of intact Self-Esteem so young people know and experience their own dignity and respect. Children, as well as adults, can only give what has been given to them, nothing more. They cannot give what they do not have. Their behavior is an indication of how we adults, and our present society, value children.

Encourage your community to create an intact Self-Esteem educational and societal environment where people can thrive **and then, watch what happens!**

> *"I now encourage everyone to create an intact Self-Esteem environment where students can thrive."*

Do You Invest In Continuing Education?

Do you remember your graduation from the 8th grade, high school, college, graduate school or post graduate school? Did you think your learning was now over? *Webster's Dictionary* defines *graduation* as a time when a person is given a degree or diploma in recognition of the completion of a course of study at a school or college.

Take a moment now to review the bodies of knowledge you have acquired or mastered so far in your life. Research shows to be a well-rounded, fully functional, multidimensional, fulfilled person you need to invest in seven bodies of knowledge for a lifetime. These include: Spiritual, Financial, Social, Mental, Physical, Family and Career.

How many courses or seminars have you attended since you graduated? How many books have you read? Have you listened to educational audiotapes weekly? I believe the most fulfilled people love to read, listen to educational audiocassettes, go to seminars and upgrade their skills daily.

When was the last time you visited a library or bookstore and explored the worlds of great ideas and great minds? By reading 20 minutes every day for six months on a specific subject, you can become an expert. The person with the skill has the power, and the person with the power has the skill. Knowledge is power. I believe when you combine your knowledge and use it with integrity, you are destined for greatness.

I believe we all need to invest daily in at least five skills in order to survive in the future and release our full potential. I also believe when your Self-Esteem is intact, you will invest more in such skills as Self-Esteem, asking questions, listening, speaking, reading, writing, math and responsibility. When you accept responsibility for everything you think, say, do and *feel*, you will create your life the way you want it. You will invest in learning more. You will know how to apply the necessary skills, at the appropriate time, thereby obtaining the best out-comes. The more you know—the more you know you don't know. Make learning fun!

Many TV's are on for hours every day. We are generally passive and nonproductive during this time.

Give yourself a grade, A – B – C – D – F, on your *Lifelong Learning Program*. Would you be interested in earning a better grade?

Decide to invest in your Lifelong Learning daily **and then, watch what happens!**

> *"I now evaluate my education and take action today to develop new skills."*

What Do You Want To "BE" When You Grow Up?

When you were in school, did anyone ever ask you, "What do you want to be when you grow up?" Are you still asking that question? People call me every day to receive career direction because they do not know how to identify or develop their uniqueness. As students graduate from college, most never use the specific knowledge they acquired. Most will have a minimum of five careers in their life time. They will need a multitude of skills in order to survive and be successful in the workplace.

Few have prepared themselves for the "what ifs" in their lives. Few people would accept the invitation to interview 25 companies before they take their first job. Few realize the resume and cover letter is an obsolete way to be hired. Few are outstanding workers. Few ever took a course in external listening, the Art of Asking Questions, presentation skills, attitudes or Self-Esteem. Few people are properly prepared to enter the work world. Few know how to motivate themselves or how to be self-starters. Few have great conversation skills. Few have a mentor to help them direct their career success.

In the future, workers will be held more accountable for their performance. They will need to be more creative. As the technology expands, they will need to be open to invest in new skills. Trades and professions will emerge that we have not even fathomed. Note how many businesses have been created as the result of society's interest in cars, exploring space, appliances and computers. What new adventures lie ahead that will create a world that, at present, is not existing?

Larry Wilson, a professional speaker, creative entrepreneur, and author of *Changing The Game: The New Way To Sell* says, "Creative mature persons are flexible. They like to play with ideas. They are open and not defensive. They are sensitive and have empathy for all people's thoughts and *feelings*. They are independent and think for themselves. They are realistic and persistent and never give up. They are foreseeing and have a long term perspective. They are expressive and spontaneous. They are curious and ask many questions. They are self accepting and believe in themselves."

Share these ideas with others **and then, watch what happens!**

> *"I now decide and help others decide what we want to BE when we grow up."*

Are You Educated To Achieve?

When was the last time you wrote down your achievements? Take a few minutes now and list your achievements. Did you complete grade school, high school, college, graduate school or postgraduate school? Did you participate in extracurricular activities? What sports do you play well? What are your communication skills? Is your Self-Esteem intact? How many friends do you have? Are you healthy? Are you drug-free? Do you depend on others for your well-being? Do you have a Lifelong Learning Program? Are you fulfilled in your work? How are your relationships? Do you have excellent people skills?

My son, Bill McGrane III, once spoke to the Ohio Department of Education about the importance of trusting and achieving. Self-Esteem is the bottom line to build trust and to achieve at the highest level of your potential. Perry Pascarella in his book, *The New Achievers*, said, "Today people want personal fulfillment at work even more than money and titles. Some companies which encourage this trend achieve remarkable results."

How is this done? First, each person and each company needs to ask the questions, "What do I want? What would having that do for me"? The answer to these questions brings clarity to decision making and achievement. The family, religion, corporations, TV, movies, magazines, books and newspapers influence what people want.

I believe, based on what is happening in society, that education has the key influence on what people want and their level of trust and achievement. What does it mean to be educated to achieve? Here are 11 questions to help you discover the answer.

1. Do you have salable, specialized skills you can use to earn an excellent income?
2. Have you learned how to learn and are you aware of your learning style?
3. Do you have a thirst for knowledge and a hunger for learning?

4. Can you communicate? What are your external listening and Art of Asking Questions skills?
5. Have you developed a clear set of values and ideals to guide your life and your daily living?
6. Do you respect the opinions of others?
7. Have you educated your *feelings?* Are you aware of *feelings* and can you describe them?
8. What is the state of your mental health?
9. Are you economically literate?
10. Do you know yourself?
11. Do you have intact Self-Esteem?

If you want to achieve your full potential, focus on educating yourself **and then, watch what happens!**

> *"I now focus on educating myself to achieve at the greatest of my potential."*

Can You Give and Teach Affirmation?

Have you noticed what is happening in education? Are you aware of the importance of teaching values to children? Do you know about the high cost of education? What about teachers? What is their responsibility?

The value of a competent teacher is priceless. In the book, *The One Minute Teacher*, Constance Johnson said, "Every one of us is both a student and a teacher. We are at our best when we each teach ourselves what we need to learn. We need to take one minute several times a day to teach ourselves what we want to learn."

Each morning take one minute and write down how you want to *be*. Write this in the form of an affirmation. An affirmation is a declaration to set in motion a way of *being*. Affirmation comes from the Latin *affirmare* and means to make firm. Conrad Baars in his book, *Born Only Once* says, "Affirmation is first of all a state of *being;* it is affectivity, a matter of *feeling.* Only secondarily is it effectivity, a matter of *doing.* Affirmation is a gift freely given with no strings attached." Thomas Aquinas said, "Man does not know the full truth until his *feelings* 'know' what his intellect knows." Thomas Kane, in his book, *Happy Are You Who Affirm* says, "The healing touch of affirmation means I encourage persons to be who they are, immaturity and short-comings included, so that their potential may BE realized."

Before writing your affirmations, I encourage you to become aware of your *feelings.* If you find it difficult to be in touch with your *feelings*—relax. Our society has taught you well! Society basically teaches us to ignore our *feelings.*

Let me assist you in discovering how you really want to *be.* Picture yourself on your deathbed reviewing your life. What do you want to leave behind to grow? Is there anything you wish you would have done differently? If you could *be* any other way what would that look like, sound like and *feel* like? How are you *being* every day? What has that state of *being* done for you in your life? How has it affected others? Remember, we are all human *Beings* and our society is constantly requesting that we *Be* human doings. The question being asked constantly in a variety of ways is, "What have you done for me lately?" If you fall into society's trap, you will constantly be *doing* to try to have and *be.* You will have a very difficult time *being* fulfilled. Pay attention to your *feelings* in conjunction with your intellect, which will let you know how to *be,* so you can do and have. When you *be* you, then you can learn exactly what to do so you can have your ideal lifestyle. You are then on the road to fulfillment.

Write your morning affirmations with *feelings,* in the present tense and specific. For example, "I now give myself permission to describe my *feelings* and *be* me." or "I now use the computer daily." With some affirmations, such as the one for the computer use, you want to set a specific date to achieve what you want. It is also important to read your affirmations often, one to three times daily.

The second part of *The One Minute Teacher* talks about the importance of catching yourself doing something correctly. Celebrate your success immediately. I believe every parent and teacher needs to give applause, compliments and recognition to every child each day. You can only give what you have. My observation is that most people do not receive compliments, therefore, they do not give compliments. A compliment is an expression of admiration, to congratulate.

Decide now to compliment five people a day. Visualize yourself now giving five individuals specific recognition. Hear the exact words you want to use and then take action. Start a journal specifically to write down the names of the people you complimented. Note the affirmation given and their reaction.

Learn to be an affirmer **and then, watch what happens!**

> *"I now take one minute to teach myself to BE an affirmer."*

Are You Learning And Fulfilled?

School days, school days, dear old golden rule days. Do you remember your first day of school? Do you recall the name of your first teacher? How clear are those pictures of a very special school event? How many years did you attend formal school? What was your greatest learning experience? How are you using what you learned? If you had it to do all over again, what body of knowledge would you invest in more deeply?

Abraham Maslow is one of my favorite teachers. He has had a great impact on my life personally and professionally, even though I never met him in person. He was a psychologist who studied healthy people. He also did research on what people need, want and value. Dr. Maslow created the "Pyramid of Needs" which depicts the hierarchy of human needs. Please be aware that we can be in several areas at one time during any time of our lives.

Dr. Maslow learned that, at the very basic level, all human beings are concerned about their physiological needs: food, clothing, shelter and air. This is especially true of children until age three. When the physiological needs are satisfied, people are ready to deal with their need for safety and security. This is the reason banks and insurance companies are so popular. Chronologically this would include the 3 to 10 year old. The third level of needs that people seek is acceptance: to be included, to be loved. You can observe this need with young people from the ages of 10–17. I believe these first three levels evolve automatically. Many people in our society are still attempting to meet their love needs.

The fourth level in the hierarchy of needs is Self-Esteem. I believe this is something that is consciously chosen. Self-Esteem is the self respect you *feel* for yourself. When people are willing and able to face their *feelings*, then they are ready to consciously learn about Self-Esteem. If all previous needs were met, the 17 to 24 year old would be developing his or her Self-Esteem. However, as I mentioned earlier, many people are stuck in their love needs.

The final level on Maslow's pyramid is the need for self-actualization or self-fulfillment. Dr. Maslow believed that only five percent of the population ever reached this level. Ideally, this occurs starting at age 24. However, most people are still preoccupied with meeting the first three levels.

Once people satisfy their needs, they are interested in their wants. For example, we may need transportation and buy a Volkswagen. Yet we may want a Cadillac. Wants enhance life and are culturally determined. Wants will vary from person to person. Often in our society, many people who obtain what they want discover that their wants do not give them fulfillment. They often respond, "Is that all there is?"

At the highest level of personal development we clarify our values. A value is that which is desirable of esteem for its own sake, that which is of importance to an individual. Values may be: God, love, autonomy, work, money, wisdom, friends, aesthetics, travel or family.

As you begin any new learning, are you a needs-driven person interested in things? Are you a values-driven person interested in self-fulfillment and the fulfillment of others? This is a lifelong journey.

If self-fulfillment is your choice, then may I suggest you create and enroll in your personal and career Lifelong Learning Program **and then, watch what happens!**

> *"I now review my past learning history and prepare for a future of fulfillment."*

What About Children's Peace Of Mind?

Are you watching the stress index every day? Do you see the violence? Do you hear about the homeless, murderers, wars, rapes and teenage pregnancies? Do you know anyone who lost his or her job? Do you know any recent high school or college graduates who cannot find their first job? Are you aware of high school dropouts, prejudice and literacy issues? Does this reality report sound like an overwhelming challenge?

There is a solution. The solution is Self-Esteem. Several years ago I met an outstanding teacher, Grace Pilon. For 60 years she taught children from kindergarten to 12th grade. She wrote a book, *Peace of Mind at an Early Age.* Her philosophy is that every child deserves to be treated with dignity and respect. As mentioned before, Self-Esteem is the self respect you *feel* for yourself.

Grace says if children's basic needs are satisfied in the learning process, provided by school systems, then they can live in peace and be productive human beings. She teaches children by asking them questions. At the same time she respects that everyone is smart and intelligent. Every person has intelligence in some area and is smart about something.

Grace says children's basic needs include:
1. Intellectual safety.
2. Inner order.
3. *Feeling* of his or her ability to create and organize.
4. Doing satisfying work on his or her own time and not in competition with peers.

5. *Feeling* of ease in relating to people, peers or adults.

6. A healthy sense of cooperation.

Grace Pilon believes every child possesses human powers which include:

1. Knowledge.
2. Creativity.
3. Sharpened sense and perceptual skills.
4. Mutual respect in a group.
5. Intact Self-Esteem.

Now begin practicing the Pilon Principles the McGrane Self-Esteem way:

1. I am smart! (repeat five times)
2. I am intelligent! (repeat five times)
3. Is it acceptable to make mistakes? Yes, because that is the way we learn.
4. Is it acceptable to ask for help? Yes, ask for your missing piece.
5. Is it acceptable not to learn everything now? Yes, the mind can only hold seven, plus or minus 2 pieces of information at one time.

Post these principles in your home, teach them to your children, repeat them three times a day **and then, watch what happens!**

> *"I now choose to practice the Pilon Principles the Self-Esteem way."*

How Have You Invested In Your Mind?

Who was your favorite teacher? Was it your mother, father, stepmother, stepfather, grandmother or grandfather? Was it a teacher in grade school, high school, college, graduate school or postgraduate school? Was it your children? Was it your boss or a friend? Was your favorite teacher a book, audio or videotape? Was it a TV show? Was it travel? Was it your personal history? Was it an addiction you had like alcohol, drugs, food . . . ? Was your favorite teacher a critical incident which created a significant emotional event? Just who or what was your favorite teacher?

I remember a teacher in my senior year of high school who helped me win the Public Speaking Contest. Little did I realize at the time, the profound impact this would have on my life. Now I have a career which includes professional speaking.

Review your Lifelong Learning personal history. How do you *feel* about what you have learned? What is your attitude about your education up to now? Do you have any regrets, "if onlys," or "what ifs"? Can you do anything about the past? Do you have unanswered questions around a body of knowledge that interests you? Have you visited your public library in the past twelve months? Will you do anything today to decide what you want to learn? Have you watched the educational channel on your television? Do you rent educational videos for you and your children? Will you invest 20 minutes a day for 6 months to become an expert on some subject? Do you read to your children daily? Can you get excited about learning?

Will you identify the great minds of history and decide to study their ideas? Will you decide to build your own library of books, audio, video and some music tapes so you can have instant access to cutting edge knowledge? Will you attend seminars, programs and speeches of people who share great ideas? Will you decide today to share your wisdom by teaching one person about an idea? Will you contact your favorite teacher and thank them for what you did with what you learned? Will you write to your superintendent of schools and thank him or her for his or her commitment to the profession?

Do it now **and then, watch what happens!**

> *"I now celebrate my mind by investing in a daily Lifelong Learning Program."*

Are You A Lifelong Learner?

What are your plans this summer? Are you going on vacation? What are your learning plans? Do you have a Lifelong Learning Program for personal enjoyment and professional success?

John Naisbitt, a futurist and author of *Megatrends* and *Global Paradox*, said, "In a world that is constantly changing, there is no one subject or set of subjects that will serve you for the foreseeable future, let alone for the rest of your life."

The most important skill to acquire now is learning how to learn. A fun way to do this is to read or listen to the quotations of famous people. Here are a few for you to review:

"Learning can be defined as the process of remembering what you are interested in."—Richard Wurman

"Anyone who stops learning is old whether at twenty or eighty. Anyone who keeps learning stays young. The greatest thing in life is to keep your mind young."—Henry Ford

"The illiterate of the year 2000 will not be the individual who cannot read or write—rather it is the one who cannot learn, unlearn, and relearn."—Alvin Toffler

"All human beings, by nature, desire to know."—Aristotle

"Cultivate your faith in yourself as a learner. Research shows that adults are better learners than children if they have the patience to be beginners."—Marilyn Ferguson

"Everyone who rises above the common level has received two educations: the first from teachers and the second, more personal and important, from yourself."—Edward Gibbon

"You learn as much by writing as you do by reading." —Eric Hoffer

"In general, the left hemisphere is more important for language and certain motor skills. On average, the right side of the brain does better with certain kinds of spatial functioning that don't depend on verbal descriptions."—Dr. Richard Restak

"One of the profound miracles of the human brain is our capacity for memory."—Jean Huston

"Self-education is the only kind of education there is. The only function of a school is to make self-education easier—failing that, it does nothing."—Isaac Asimov

May I suggest you read every day, listen to audiocassettes daily, create a personal and professional Lifelong Learning Program **and then, watch what happens!**

"I now choose to be a Lifelong Learner!"

Are You Educated For the Future?

Are you a doctor, lawyer or dentist? Have you noticed how they say, "I practice medicine," "I practice law," or "I practice dentistry"? What skills will you practice for the future? What do you want to learn to be prepared for the next 10–15 years? Bob Richards, a famous Olympian, said, "It takes 10,000 hours of skill development to prepare for the Olympics."

The world of work is changing drastically. Eighty-five percent of American workers are unfulfilled in what they do. A television celebrity who was visiting a station where he had worked for many years told me, "The stress level was explosive."

How do people prepare themselves for the "What Ifs?" of life? "What if I lose my job?" "What if my company closes or has a merger?" "What if my business goes bankrupt?" "What if I want more responsibility or more money?" "What do I need to do to get the outcome I want?" "Who do I consult about my career plans?" "Do I have or want a mentor?" "Just what is my ultimate ideal career?"

When I was teaching "Orientation to Business" at the University of Cincinnati (it really was a career Self-Esteem course), I would suggest to the students, "It is not important to know specifically where you are going. It is important to go and along the way you will find out!" Then I suggested they breathe a sigh of relief. They knew the outcome was to *get an education;* however, they did not know the specific degree or field they wanted. Students are always asked what they want to do. I believe it is more important to know what you want to BE first, then you can learn what you want to do.

The President of Xavier University once spoke at a Rotary meeting about the Jesuit system of teaching. He said, "The ideal college education begins with a liberal arts foundation. Research shows that many college graduates were taught to go to school to get a job. The Jesuits believe you go to college to learn how to think and how to make connections from one idea to another."

How will you utilize your skill development now and in the future to earn fulfillment and financial rewards? I believe fulfillment and peace of mind is 95% of life, while monetary income is only 5% of life.

This is an excellent time to examine your existing life skills. Then you can evaluate which skills can propel you to the highest level of career competency and productivity. A wise man once said, "Education is a process—not a destination." Life is also a process—not a destination.

I believe the best way to become educated is to ask yourself powerful questions. Here are 10 questions to ask yourself to determine how well you are prepared for the future.

1. Do you have a saleable, specialized skill you can sell for money?

   Your *feeling* of Self-Esteem influences where you choose to work, how productive you are, and your environment (toxic or healthy). I believe people earn up to what their Self-Esteem tells them they deserve, and I also believe they work with people and organizations based on their Self-Esteem.

2. Is your Self-Esteem intact?

   Self-Esteem is the respect you *feel* for yourself. How well do you know yourself? How balanced are you in the way you live? I believe a balanced lifestyle includes a daily investment in seven areas of life: Spiritual, Financial, Social, Mental, Physical, Family and Career.

Wheel of Life

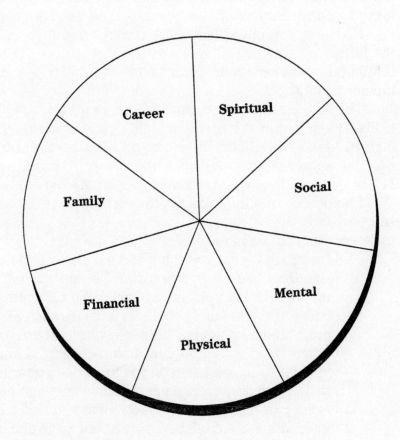

3. Have you learned how to learn?
What is your personality style, your listening style, your learning style, your value system and what are your persuasive skills? Are you left brain or right brain dominant, or are you balanced? The left brain deals with thinking and facts. The right brain is involved with *feelings* and process. Are you content- or process-oriented? Content is the specifics, the data, the information, the meat. Process is any phenomenon which shows a continuous change in time, a series of actions or operations definitely leading to an end. It's a continuing development involving many changes.

4. Do you have a thirst for knowledge and a hunger for learning?
As a child you were probably very curious. Gradually you may have lost your childlike curiosity and stopped asking questions. Do you read a book a week? Do you subscribe to your career periodical? Do you invest at least 10% of your income in your brain? The future will demand multiple skill development.

5. Can you communicate?
Do you say what you think and *feel* easily and understandably? Are you articulate? Do you have a love for words? Do you use affirming Self-Esteem language? Do you label people with names such as "stupid," "idiot" or "moron"? People who criticize or put others down have crippling, unintact Self-Esteem. Do you guarantee each person you meet that you will call them by their correct name which helps them have a *feeling* of dignity and respect? Give yourself a communication test. Today stop using language that hurts such as "should," "ought" and "must." These words are damaging to Self-Esteem. They can be replaced with "need," "want" and "consider." How do you communicate nonverbally? Give the next five people you meet a hug and watch what happens (ask permission first).

6. Have you developed a clear set of values and principles to guide your life and daily living?

   Are you outer-directed or inner-directed? I believe inner-directed people demonstrate less distress because they are acting from the inside out. They are more other-centered then self-centered. Outer-directed people take their direction from everyone except themselves. They rarely discover who they really are and what they really want. They are too busy doing what everyone else wants.

7. Have you learned how to respond to people who challenge your ideas or values?

   Do you give people undivided attention when they criticize your behavior? With intact Self-Esteem, you encourage people to freely describe their *feelings* instantly when there is conflict. You do not take things personally.

8. Have you educated your *feelings?*

   Do you appreciate fine music, great art, classic literature and the sights and sounds of nature? A quality lifestyle includes "five sensing" every experience: using sight, sound, taste, touch and smell to "experience-the-experience-of-the-experience." The deeper our *feelings*, the more we ground each experience. To ground is to bring it down from the realm of ideas into the realm of daily life.

9. What is the state of your mental health?

   How many days were you sick last year? What are your sick habits? What are your health habits? What are your Self-Esteem habits? How does intact Self-Esteem affect your mental health? Discuss these questions with your family and friends. What is an affirming Self-Esteem lifestyle?

10. Are you economically literate?

    What do you know about financial planning? Money management can be challenging. Do you have a financial planning mentor? Do you take courses on business competence? Do you have a Lifelong Learning fund?

There you have it—10 ideas for you to process now and in the future to maximize your full potential. So, like the doctors, lawyers and dentists, we need to practice, practice, practice! The Japanese have a word for the process—it is "Kaizen," which means incremental improvement.

I support and encourage you in your journey to create an affirming Self-Esteem lifestyle. With intact Self-Esteem, happiness and success are inevitable!

Educate yourself for the future **and then, watch what happens!**

"I now educate myself for the future."

Chapter Four

Family

Is Your Family In Distress Or Harmony?

Have you noticed all the people talking about stress and distress, especially family stress? Families are not supposed to be the source of stress. Ideally, families provide a place of peace and harmony where we recoup from the pressures of the outside world. It is a place to gather new energy to put back into our jobs or businesses. Because family stress is spilling over into society, it is beginning to receive some attention. Time pressures on families in which both parents work are affecting the job performances of these men and women.

At least 75% of the Fortune 500 companies now have marriage and family professionals on staff because employees are bringing family related problems to work. Delores Curran, in her book, *Stress and the Healthy Family*, defines family distress as a condition that exists when family life gets out of control. Symptoms of a constantly stressful family include:

1. Constant sense of urgency and hurry.
2. No time to release and relax.
3. Tension that underlies and causes sharp words.
4. Sibling fighting and value judging (comparing values to find their agreement or disagreement).
5. A mania to escape to one's room, car or garage to get away from it all.
6. *Feelings* of frustration over not getting things done.
7. A pervasive sense of guilt for not being and doing everything to and for all people in one's life.

The top ten stresses for families in order of priority are listed below.

1. Economics, finances and budgeting.
2. Children's behavior, discipline and sibling fighting.
3. Insufficient couple time.
4. Lack of shared responsibility in the family.
5. Communicating with children.
6. Insufficient "ME" time.
7. Guilt for not accomplishing more.
8. Spouse communication.

9. Insufficient family play time.

10. Over-scheduled family calendar.

What is the solution to family distress? Self-Esteem is the bottom line. When both husband and wife model the behavior of intact Self-Esteem, the children can better learn how to create balance in their lives. Mom and Dad need to first make time for themselves as individuals—then as a couple—so they can be present to each child and then the family. A parent can only give what they have and nothing more.

May I suggest you build your Self-Esteem daily **and then, watch what happens!**

> *"I now choose family harmony*
> *by building Self-Esteem."*

What Is Laser Beam T.U.A.?

Have you ever seen a laser light show? People are fascinated by the power of the laser and the mirrors that bounce the light to a new location. The *Webster's Dictionary* defines the laser as "a device containing a crystal, gas or other suitable substance in which atoms, when stimulated by focused light waves, emit them in a narrow very intense beam."

As I have watched people enjoying laser shows, I wondered, "What attractions or special events have the power to get people's attention to take action?" Certainly holidays—like Mother's Day—will increase greeting card sales, flower sales, restaurant sales and family gatherings.

During all my years as a Self-Esteem Consultant, I have shared with all groups that, "We never get over our mother or father." We always want a meaningful relationship with our parents (or other caretakers). Their parenting may or may not have been what you wanted. Yet, they did the best they could with the knowledge and skills they possessed. Parents are not perfect in their behavior. They make mistakes just like you do. Be appreciative of the gifts they gave you, especially the gift of life!

May I encourage you to zero-in like a laser beam on your mother if she is still alive. If she has already left this world, pause a moment to appreciate her impact on you. Do that now. Hold your hand out in front of you with the palm toward you and pretend it is your mother's palm. A mother is often the first person to hold and hug you. Your mother may have been the first person to give you Self-Esteem. A mother might have been the first person to accept you Totally and Unconditionally. That is the reason the McGrane Self-Esteem Institute definition for Self-Esteem is T.U.A. (Total Unconditional Acceptance). A mother may have been the first person to experience new changes in your growth and development. A mother was the first person you ran to and said, "Look Mom—I did it all by myself."

So each day as you use your hands to take action, ask yourself, "Is that a Self-Esteem choice?" Remember, all of us were born with intact Self-Esteem.

This week remember your mother as a laser beam who focused on you with T.U.A. **and then, watch what happens!**

> *"I now act like a laser beam and give five people T.U.A."*

Do You Have Parent Burnout?

Have you heard of the book, *Parent Burnout?* I heard the author describe parent burnout. Many parents are worn out; they are tired of raising children; they want time for themselves; and they would like help. This behavior is the result of all of the pressures parents *feel* as they live their lives.

Today, many women work at their careers, then they come home to cook, take care of the house, and find little time for themselves. Many children are abused because of these pressures and could be damaged for a lifetime. Our greatest asset is our children! Our future and the future of our country lies in their hands. How we serve them now will determine how we will be served later.

There is a man who was a recovering alcoholic. He had three daughters. When he was drinking, he verbally abused his children. He called them names and yelled at them. When a child is called all kinds of labels like "stupid" or yelled at, the impact is devastating.

As I meet people during our Self-Esteem programs, I always hear about parents who affected their children in a non-affirming way. One person told me, "When I was 23 years old, my father said to me, "I am disappointed in you." From that moment, the young man wanted nothing to do with his father. Another woman was told by her father, "You aren't worth the time it took to make you." These words cut deeper than a knife.

How can we create a home environment where children can thrive? How can we build the Self-Esteem of parents and children so that there is harmony and cooperation at home? What can parents do to pamper themselves to prevent parent burnout?

Decide that children are a gift. Value children even when their behavior is unacceptable. Give children instant consequences for unacceptable behavior—free of guilt, blame and punishment. For example, if a child marks up a wall with crayons say, "Sammy that is unacceptable behavior. Crayons are for paper or your coloring book. The consequence for marking on the wall is you need to clean the crayon off the wall." Say this with your normal voice, with no anger or disappointment. Then, no matter what the child's age is, have him or her scrub the crayon off the wall.

Prepare children for life by giving them direction. Create calmness in the home. Most of all give yourself, as a parent, a minimum of 30 minutes of quiet time each day. Find a mentor to talk with daily. Share these ideas with other parents. With intact Self-Esteem you take care of your needs and then there is no parent burnout.

Take action now **and then, watch what happens!**

> *"I now take 30 minutes of quiet time daily to
> prepare myself for my total fulfillment."*

Do You Appreciate Laura And Children?

Do you know Bill McGrane III? Bill III is a part of the McGrane Self-Esteem Institute and is spreading the Self-Esteem message to individuals and corporations every day. Well—So What! The "So What" is that a new person has joined the McGrane family. Her name is Laura Longworth McGrane— a beautiful new baby!

I had the privilege and pleasure of holding her three days after she was born and had her listen to her first music. The song was Laura, one of my favorite songs. I played it several times for her. It may become her theme song.

As I held Laura in my arms, I thought of how dependent she is on her parents and others to feed and love her, until she becomes self-sufficient. I thought of how her parents will create a Self-Esteem environment where she can thrive. I thought about the power of touch. Virginia Satir, a family therapist, believes that touching creates healing and a *feeling* of calmness and tranquillity.

As a grandfather, I will cherish the magic moments Laura will create for people as she grows and gradually takes charge of her life. Laura is born into a world of acceptance and challenge. People with intact Self-Esteem will accept Laura and help her develop her Self-Esteem.

When she stays in an intact Self-Esteem home, she is safe from criticism, put downs, blame, guilt and child abuse, physical and emotional. As she meets new people, she will meet many challenges with people whose Self-Esteem is not intact.

As Laura develops, she will create a climate of love and acceptance with every person she meets. Children will want to play with her. Adults will learn to *feel* more important when they meet her. Laura will expand her competence, free from comparing herself to others. She will avoid self-image behavior, such as acting as if she is better than other people. She will develop her skills daily to maximize her potential.

So now we meet Laura, my new beautiful granddaughter. She will call me Grandfather. I will enjoy watching Laura learn and develop intact Self-Esteem behavior.

I thank God for Laura, and I will affirm her to be the best that she can be, and you can do the same for children you know, **and then, watch what happens!**

> *"I now appreciate all children and help them acquire intact Self-Esteem."*

Are You Preparing Teens For Life?

Do you have trouble understanding teenagers? Do you remember your teenage years? Seven powerful years make up the teen experience.

Teenagers want to be accepted and included. They want to be part of the group. Peer pressure is the big challenge to survival in the teen years. What are some of the issues? A few of the pressures include: cars, sports success, college acceptance, acquiring all the best and most current clothes and being invited to the "in" parties. What about other issues like: alcohol, drugs, exercise, nutrition, getting along with parents, summer jobs, boredom in school, school dropouts, both parents working and a hunger for friendship?

So how do we communicate with teenagers for seven years to prepare them for life? How do we speak their language? Teenagers have their own language. We need to learn everyone's language if we want to communicate at the highest level. However, teen language changes from day to day. How do we keep current? Advertisers need to appeal to teenagers, so research discovers the new language, to guarantee billions of dollars of product sales.

Teenagers learn the language so they can survive those seven trying years. I believe we need to teach Self-Esteem language to teens. Would you like to learn a universal Self-

Esteem language to help your communication skills? Are you interested in releasing words that can cut to the core of a person's Self-Esteem? Is it important for you to model behavior that can serve you and your teenagers? Are you willing to practice even if your teenager chooses not to participate?

You can begin by eliminating three words. These words can be harmful to your and others' Self-Esteem because they set people up for comparison. Comparison destroys Self-Esteem. The three words you want to begin releasing from your vocabulary are "Should," "Ought" and "Must." Have you or your teenager ever been told, "You should do this. You ought to do that. You must do it this way"? The replacement for these words are: "Need", "Want" and "Consider".

Test these words for the next 30 days **and then, watch what happens!**

> *"I now learn Self-Esteem language to prepare teenagers for life."*

Do You Recall Special Moments With Your Mother?

What is the first *feeling* you experience when you hear the word *Mother?* Are they sad *feelings* or happy *feelings?* Recall the happiest moments with your mother and write them down. Are they big events or simple moments that only you and she know?

A newspaper once invited 75 fourth and fifth grade children to choose words they most like to hear from their mothers.

Here are five top choices repeated over and over by almost all of the children.

1. I love you.
2. Yes.
3. Time to eat.
4. You can go.
5. You can stay up late.

Here are some other favorites.

1. I'll help you.
2. You are special.
3. Let's go to the movie.
4. You don't have to clean your room.
5. Let's go for a walk.
6. I appreciate your helping me clean the kitchen.
7. Your friend can spend the night.
8. You can go out and play.
9. I'm happy you came to our house to live.
10. I have a surprise for you.
11. Thank you.
12. I know you can do it.

What did the fourth and fifth grade children list as the things they did not like their mothers to say?

1. How many times do I have to tell you . . .?
2. I am disappointed in you.
3. Ask your father.
4. You will never amount to anything.
5. I'm ashamed of you.
6. Don't argue with me.
7. Why can't you be like your brother or sister?

I believe your mother makes a profound impact on your life. If your mother was loved, she taught you how to love. If your mother was hugged, she taught you to hug.

This week, recall the happy moments with your mother. If your mother is alive, write her a love letter, send her a card, buy her a rose and say, "A rose says it all." Tell her you love her and give her a hug.

If your mother is not with you, close your eyes, recall the happiest moment you ever experienced, relish that moment, and experience those special *feelings* **and then, watch what happens!**

> **"I now recall special happy moments with my mother."**

Do You Love Your Father?

How would you describe your father? What qualities of his are important to you? What do you like least about your father? What qualities do you like best? When you were a child, did your father push you on a swing, play ball with you or watch you play sports? Did he go to PTA (Parent–Teacher Association) meetings or encourage you when you brought home a poor report card? Did he teach you any sport, or to ride a bike, or to drive a car? Did he help you learn a difficult subject?

Did he hold you on his lap when you were a child? Did he tell you stories or read to you? Did he hug you and tell you, "I love you"? Did he ever write you a letter? Did he take you on vacation?

On Father's Day we show our love to our fathers. If your father is not available, can you remember him for his special unique qualities? If your father is alive, how will you celebrate Father's Day? Will you call him on the telephone or visit him? Will you write a special letter or ask him, "What it is like to be a father?" Will you thank him for being your father? Will you forgive him for any behavior that made you uncomfortable? Will you decide to improve your relationship with him? Will you commit to talk with your father at least once a week? Will you recognize the skills and qualities you received from him? Are you interested in receiving more?

How well do you know your father? Have you asked him about his childhood years? How was he parented and what did he like best and least about that parenting? What were his greatest challenges in his life? What are his feelings about being a father? Who are his heroes and role models? What are his top five skills and values? What kinds of jobs or businesses has he had? What does he like best about himself?

Millions of Father's Day cards will be bought this year. Most of the cards will have words written by another person. What would need to exist to write your own message to your father? Consider writing him a love letter and thanking him for being your dad. Also include the characteristics you like best about him in the letter.

Every father creates a lifetime impact. Women want a man to have inner strength and compassion. When you call or write your dad, give him the best Father's Day gift he could ever receive—just say, "Dad, I love you!" **and then, watch what happens!**

> *"I now find it easier to tell my father I love him."*

Do You Dare?

Did anyone ever say to you, "I dare you. I double dare you."? Did they say, "I dare you to skip school. I dare you to hit me."? Did anyone ever dare you to smoke, drink alcohol or take drugs?

What answers did you give to "I dare yous"? What habits do you have today because you accepted or refused to accept a dare? How did you *feel* when you accepted a dare, and how did you *feel* when you refused a dare? Were you laughed at and put down? Did your peers reject you and make fun of you? If you were a young person today, would you be able to handle the pressures they face?

When young people today are invited to accept a dare, many of them are addicted for a lifetime. Peer pressure is very powerful. Rejection feels terrible and painful. Young people want to be accepted, included and be part of the "in" group. They have so many choices and are unsure which direction will best meet their needs.

What can we do to make it easier for our youth to say "No" and *feel* in charge of their lives? Prevention is the key. Helping them to have intact Self-Esteem is the solution. One way to do that is to say to them, "I dare you who come from a home of poverty to have the qualities of Lincoln." "I dare you wealthy person to give yourself away by finding a cause bigger than life." "I dare you young mother to make your life a masterpiece upon which that little family of yours can build intact Self-Esteem." "I dare you boys and girls to say "No" to smoking, vandalism, alcohol and drugs." "I dare you young executive to accept more responsibility and maximize your potential." "I dare you young author to win the Nobel Peace Prize." "I dare you young researcher to find a cure for cancer." "I dare you boy or girl on the farm to become a master farmer—a hunger fighter." "I dare you to have a magnificent obsession." "I dare you retired person to share your wisdom with the world." "I dare you to catch a passion for helping others, and a richer life will come back to you."

I dare you to buy the book *I Dare You* by William H. Danforth. I dare you to read the book yourself. Next I dare you to give it to a young person **and then, watch what happens!**

> *"I now accept a dare to invest*
> *in the book I Dare You."*

Do You Support And Encourage?

Have you heard about a Gallop poll about families? Mr. Gallop says the family used to be the comfortable nest that accepted you, in spite of your behavior, with uncritical, undemanding love. At least that's the way it was supposed to be. The new Gallop poll now says just the opposite.

The family is now the primary agent of personal change. It is the energy source to get us unstuck from smoking, alcohol, drugs, obesity or other unhealthy habits, and help us live at our best. When it comes to health, most people get help from their family more than any other source. Some people are finding that their family gives them the power and the push to be the best they can be.

Gallop asked members of families, "Who helped you change?" Most people said a significant member of their family had the greatest influence on helping them change a particular health habit such as quitting smoking, cutting down on alcohol, controlling job stresses, exercising more, losing weight or eating healthier. The Gallop poll shows that family and loved ones help us shape our health habits more than doctors do.

The *American Health* magazine asked for the Gallop research on family health. They found that many people *feel* they do not deserve support and encouragement—even from family members. Also, some women find their husbands give them less help than they would like.

In the 1950's and '60's we became the "Me" generation. Now we are the "Us" generation. When family members work for each others' well-being, they create a family at its best! When their health is at stake, the family that supports each other can grow healthier together. Is there anyone in your family who needs to be supported with a health issue? How can you serve them? What can you do to help them discover the best choice for the outcomes they want?

Is there anyone in your extended family that is dealing with some challenges? What about your: Work family? Social family? Play family?

The guaranteed way to give support is to create a Self-Esteem environment where members of the family can thrive **and then, watch what happens!**

> *"I now give support and encouragement to each family member."*

Is Your Family Environment Healthy?

As you read the previous messages, do you recall the ideas about stress in the family and the consequences? Dolores Curran says that stress effective families are more interested in relationships rather than in behavior and discipline.

Almost all of the traits identified in healthy families are relational. When they exist there is less need for discipline. Discipline is a tool used to establish and correct behaviors. *When relationships are healthy, behaviors tend to be healthy.*

When relationships are unhealthy, the best disciplinary techniques will not be effective in establishing Self-Esteem behaviors.

Below are 14 traits of a healthy family that Delores Curran mentions in her book, *Stress and the Healthy Family.*

1. Healthy families communicate and listen.
2. Healthy families affirm and support.
3. Healthy families respect one another.
4. Healthy families develop trust.
5. Healthy families have a sense of play and humor.
6. Healthy families share responsibilities.
7. Healthy families identify acceptable and unacceptable behavior.
8. Healthy families build a sense of family.
9. Healthy families have a balance of interaction.
10. Healthy families have a shared religious core.
11. Healthy families respect privacy.
12. Healthy families foster table time and conversation.
13. Healthy families share leisure time.
14. Healthy families admit to challenges and ask for help.

Notice how many of these traits are relationship oriented. When a family successfully develops half of these traits, they don't need many disciplinary techniques. When members of a family can communicate and listen to each other, they are already working through situations which would otherwise require discipline. Modeling the behavior of a healthy family is the best way to develop and enhance your family relationships.

Building Self-Esteem is the key to family harmony. Affirm your family daily **and then, watch what happens!**

> *"I now choose to create a healthy
> family environment."*

Chapter Five

Holidays

Are You Interested In Giving Thanks?

What are your plans for Thanksgiving? Will you invite your family to your home? Will you visit your parents? Will you be with friends? Will you go on a trip? Will you be alone? How did you *feel* when you read, "Will you be alone?"

Observe the behavior of the individuals sitting around the Thanksgiving dinner table. Are you able to discover who has been nibbled at during their lifetime? This could be a family member, friend or stranger. We all nibble at food or take big bites. Let's focus on how people have been nibbled at and possibly had their Self-Esteem destroyed.

Do you recognize the person who was criticized, put down or labeled as dumb or incompetent? Do you see someone who is thin or fat? Can you recognize if they were made to *feel* "less than"? Look at peoples' clothing, their car or their house. Do they accept where they are or do they compare themselves to those who have more?

Thanksgiving is meant to be a time for abundance: abundance of food, health, friendship, appreciation, conversation, family and love. How will you give abundance this week to everyone you meet and to those with whom you celebrate Thanksgiving?

When you complete your dinner and you are comfortable, turn to the person on your right and say, "I appreciate your friendship," or "I want to thank you for making it important enough to be here for our family celebration," or "I appreciate how you were available for me when I wanted you to listen to me." Then encourage the others to turn to the individual on their right and share something they appreciate. Do it all around the table. When you are affirmed, turn to the person on your left and begin the process again. It could be the most memorable Thanksgiving experience of your life.

Some people could be uncomfortable and may not want to participate. Allow them to pass and continue the process. You may discover they will participate toward the end or may say something privately to someone later in the evening. Every person has his or her own timing. Be sensitive to each person by creating a climate of acceptance. The outcome is to model

intact Self-Esteem behavior and have as many people participate by giving and receiving two affirmations.

When the affirmations are complete, give everyone a big
Self-Esteem hug **and then, watch what happens!**

> *"I now give the gift of Self-Esteem*
> *to each member of my family."*

Are You A Nibbler?

Have you started your holiday shopping? Do you like to
give presents to people? Do you like to receive gifts from
people? Do you prefer tangible or intangible gifts? Do you want
a gift to last a short time or a long time? Have you ever received
a gift that would last a lifetime? What would need to exist for
you to receive a gift from yourself that would last a lifetime and
give a gift to others that would last a lifetime?

When I was born, I was given the gift of Self-Esteem which
could last a lifetime. However, I did not know how to take care
of it. My gift was nibbled at daily by different people! Some
people said I was "dumb." Others said, "You can't do that."
Someone said, "Be careful, you 'should' be afraid, you can't
learn that." I heard many of those statements over and over
again and gradually I believed them. I was afraid to speak to
people, afraid to raise my hand in class, and afraid to learn. I
felt other people were smarter than I. I held back from fulfilling
my potential because of all the nibbles.

For more than 40 years I asked the question, "How come
people hurt so much and nibble at each other?" It took all that
time to discover that it was a Self-Esteem issue. In 1976 I
met L. S. Barksdale who knew how to stop others and himself
from hurting and nibbling.

In January of 1985, I met Kaleel Jamison, an Organizational Development Consultant. She observed all the nibbles

people were receiving. Some nibbles include: "You ask too many questions." "You work too hard." "You're too frank." "You're too helpful." A nibble asks you to make yourself less powerful. Kaleel wanted people to release nibbles so she wrote a book called *The Nibble Theory*. There are only 74 pages in this book. It is a book about leadership, self-empowerment and personal development. Kaleel talks about your kernel of power. She notes, "That kernel, that central part of you, that self, is your source of joy and serenity. It is also where you find balance, respect, competence, stability and power." I believe that kernel of power is your Self-Esteem. *The Nibble Theory* is one of the most powerful books I have ever read. Clothes wear out and food is consumed. Yet a book can bring happiness for a lifetime.

Give yourself the lifetime gift of releasing nibbles **and then, watch what happens!**

> *"I now stop nibbling at my own and others' Self-Esteem."*

How Is Your Courage?

What could be the best gift to give yourself when you begin a new year? People get excited about many things during this time of year. What was your best gift in the past year? How much closer are you to fulfillment, peace of mind and tranquillity? Do you live a balanced lifestyle: spiritually, financially, socially, mentally, physically, family and career?

Great changes are taking place in the world every day. What would be a powerful word for next year and future years? The word I suggest to you is "courage." *Courage* is not the absence of fear. Webster defines *courage* as "that quality of mind which enables one to meet danger and difficulties with firmness, valor." Author Sidney Bremer says, "Courage is the brother to decisions." True courage is cool and calm. Peter Marshall, author and minister, said, "God give us the courage to stand for something lest we fall for anything."

So let's look at the word *COURAGE* as an acrostic (describing the use of a word by having each letter stand for another word or phrase) for the next year.

C—reminds us that it takes courage to *communicate*—verbally, nonverbally and tactually. It takes courage to listen, to ask questions and to give undivided attention to everyone we meet.

O—reminds us to be *open* to ideas, conversation and every life event. Stretch to new levels of awareness.

R—reminds us to be *responsible* for everything we think, say, do and *feel*. With intact Self-Esteem, we choose language to help people *feel* better about themselves. It takes courage to not defend, justify or explain your behavior.

A—reminds us about our *attitudes*. Our attitude is the way we think.

G—reminds us to *grow*. How many books will you read in the next year to upgrade your people skills? How many learning programs/seminars will you attend? How many cassettes will you listen to?

E—reminds us of our *Esteem*. Self-Esteem is the self respect you *feel* for yourself. It takes courage to practice your Self-Esteem skills. Many people are threatened when you change.

Were you aware I left out the letter "U" until now? The reason I did that was to remind *you* that *you* depend on *you* to show *courage*.

This is my gift to you for the next year—the gift of courage. I wish you the courage to create intact Self-Esteem daily.

Let us create peace on earth by showing courage every day in everything we think, say, do and *feel* **and then, watch what happens!**

> *"I now choose to have the courage
> to take charge of my life."*

Have You Given Food?

Do you like food? I do! We have thousands of choices. Each choice has an outcome, a consequence. Some foods are loaded with calories while other foods are light in calories. At least three times a day our brain triggers a desire to eat food. In our lifetime we could eat at least 100,000 times. We are constantly being encouraged to make healthy food choices and to inspect what we eat like a customs house.

Research shows our health is related to what we eat. I recently listened to some women who were victims of the disease, anorexia nervosa. They chose to stop eating because they *felt* they were too fat. They had developed the "perfection" syndrome. They *felt* they had to have a perfect body, perfect grades, perfect friends, perfect marriage and a perfect job. Everything had to be perfect!

As I listened, these women said they had to be in control. Since they *felt* they could not control many parts of their life, at least they could control how much food they ate. The end result was, in their desire to be in control, they lost control, even with the possibility of death. This behavior is another example of unintact Self-Esteem choices.

Eighty-eight million people every day wake up preoccupied with food choices to control their weight. We are a nation that loves food. We are bombarded with thousands of invitations to taste new foods.

Holidays are a time when the focus is on food. Family gatherings are usually centered around a special lunch or dinner. Unique desserts are available during the holidays. Many look forward to this special time of year.

Yet millions of people are hungry: physically, socially, emotionally and psychologically, and many are facing a deep crisis in their lives. What one thing can you do to share some food with one person or organization? Look around for that person, take that person to a restaurant, give them some food and talk with them. Discover their path in life. What is their personal history, skills and talents? Treat them like royalty! Remember, they were someone's baby, brother, sister, parent and so forth. When you give them nutritional food, it serves the body. When you give them T.U.A. (Total Unconditional Acceptance), it affirms them as a person and serves their Self-Esteem.

During the holidays celebrate your Self-Esteem **and then, watch what happens!**

> *"I now choose to give food to one needy person."*

Are You Interested In An Ideal Gift?

If you could choose to give an ideal gift to yourself or someone else, what would it be? Would you want to be a millionaire? And then what? Would you want to be the President of the United States? And then what? Would you want to be the most beautiful woman or most handsome man in the world? And then what? Would you want to live in the biggest mansion in the world? And then what? Would you want the most respected career in the world? And then what? Would you want friends in every country in the world? And then what? Would you want freedom from pain for the rest of your life? And then what? Would you want to love your neighbor as yourself for all of your life? And then what?

As you evaluate those questions, how do you think and *feel* about an ideal gift? We have thousands of potential choices daily. In the United States there are huge multipurpose stores where you can buy almost anything. The advertising specialists for these stores know how to create the demand for things. They know how to move things from their shelves to your home, thus becoming your possessions. Remember the year children "could not live" without Cabbage Patch Dolls? What is this year's craze?

What do you really, really, really, really, really really, really want? Do you want things that are temporary or things that are permanent? Do your want temporary or permanent relationships? Do you want a temporary or permanent career? Of all the things you buy, receive or give, which will make a lifelong impact?

A man once came to my office. He had started a new career and he was asked, "How come you changed careers"? He said, "My 13 year old son asked me to play football and I said, 'I'm too tired.' Next he asked me to play frisbee and I said, 'I'm too tired.' Then my son said, 'Dad, do you remember the song *Cats In the Cradle?*'" The man then listened to the song. The song let him know that his son was going to grow up to be just like him. Therefore, when the father would want time to be with his son, the son would reply, "I'm too busy or tired." The man realized the time to be with his son was now, and he decided to change his career. He said, "It was a Self-Esteem issue. I did not want to be on my deathbed and say, 'If only I would have. . . . "

Just what is the ideal gift to give yourself and others that will last a lifetime? Decide now to give yourself that great gift—the gift of intact Self-Esteem (a gift that only you can give yourself) **and then, watch what happens!**

> *"I now give myself the gift of intact Self-Esteem."*

Is Love Important In Your Life?

Do you receive Valentine's greetings from anyone? Did your spouse or significant other remember you on Valentine's Day? Did you remember this person? Did your children send you a special love message? Did your friends, boss or fellow employees acknowledge you?

This time of year, people send millions of cards with messages published by greeting card companies. They help many people who have a difficult time describing their own *feelings*, especially their *feelings* about love.

Self-Esteem is the respect you *feel* for yourself. Furthermore, the *feelings* you have about yourself are the *feelings* you have about other people. You can only love others based on how you love yourself. You can only give what you have and nothing more. The *Bible* says, "Love your neighbor as yourself."

We at the McGrane Self-Esteem Institute call love "T.U.A." (Total Unconditional Acceptance)—which includes everyone! This means, "I can love you; however, I may not love your behavior." When we can separate the person from his/her behavior, then we can have T.U.A.. We will then concentrate on modeling appropriate behavior for others to see.

For example—on a recent television show the subject was suicide. It was about how to recognize the symptoms and what to do about it. People on the show agreed that it is important to encourage the suicidal person to talk about his or her *feelings*. That is a way to love. Listening is loving. Asking questions is loving. Giving compliments is loving. Sending a rose to someone and saying, "A rose says it all," is loving. Sending a thank-you note is loving. Teaching someone is loving. Being present to someone (giving them your undivided attention) is loving. Visiting someone in the hospital or nursing home is loving. Writing your own *feelings* is loving.

One of my favorite teachers is Abraham Kaplan. He said this of love, "Love is commitment. Love is caring. Love is respect. Love is sharing. Love is joy. Love is growth." The ancient philosopher, Plato, said this about love, "If there were only some way of contriving that a state or an army could be made up of lovers—they would be the very best governors." "Even the army," he said, "when fighting at each others' side, although a mere handful, the lovers would overcome the war."

So focus on loving and T.U.A. **and then, watch what happens!**

> *"I now accept myself and everyone totally*
> *and unconditionally."*

What Is Love?

What does Valentine's Day mean to you? Is it a commercial day to sell candy, flowers and greeting cards? Or is it a reminder to say, "I love you!" to our loved ones? What is your definition of love? Love is T.U.A. (Total Unconditional Acceptance).

Loving implies a willingness to love someone as they are; it is not contingent on their becoming what we desire them to be. People were not put on this earth for our happiness and convenience. When we love someone we enjoy watching them accomplish the outcomes they want daily. We also enjoy when they interact successfully with others. We want them to succeed, and to find the joy and the peace they are seeking. We want them to BE all that they can BE. We do everything to enhance that possibility.

When we love someone and they love us, we *feel* comfortable with them. There is no need to always be on our best behavior to be accepted, no need for games or one-upmanship. We know we love someone when we are as willing to accept their undeveloped skills as well as we accept their developed skills. No one can satisfy our every need or be the perfect spouse, parent, friend, etc.. When we accept that fact, we stop trying to redesign each other in the name of love. Then we see more of their potential and serve them in their own self-discovery.

Our ability to love is equal to our ability to forgive. We are lovers to the degree we are willing to forgive and continue the process of loving. Forgiving is *for giving!*

People who love have intact Self-Esteem. They value everyone they meet. We can only love others based on the way we love ourselves. You can only give what you have. Love is T.U.A. (Total Unconditional Acceptance). So no matter what you think, say, do or *feel*, you are still lovable and capable—

and so is everyone else. However, you are still responsible for everything you think, say, do and *feel*—and so is everyone else. T.U.A. gives you the loving support to make mistakes, as you are in the Lifelong Learning Process. You can usually correct for error now or in the future.

Decide now to tell your mother, your father, your spouse, your children, your friends and others that you love them **and then, watch what happens!**

> *"I now give T.U.A. to everyone I meet."*

When Was The Last Time You Gave Thanks?

Do you have a job or a career? Are you satisfied or fulfilled? Can you identify the unique factor which helps you create a passion for your work? Do you like to work alone or with people? Can you identify your two most important skills? Do you upgrade your skills daily? Are there some new skills you would like to learn? Who do you know that can teach you new skills? Have you ever volunteered your skills to teach others how to take charge of their lives? Do you believe that you receive a surge of Self-Esteem when you give some of your competence, ideas or money to another person?

You become an inspiring role model as you share your skills without financial gain. Instead of money you receive fulfillment and peace of mind, which is 95% of life. Mother Teresa is an example of giving her talents and energy to the poor. Back in the 1930's she dedicated herself to be in service to the poor. She became a well renowned woman who taught by doing. She volunteered her services for a lifetime. Many people, from all over the world, helped her do her work, and as a result they found fulfillment in their lives as well.

During Thanksgiving season (or any time of the year) we can become aware of our gifts. As you think about the words *thanks* and *giving*, what thoughts come to mind? Do you hear many people say thank you for the things you do? Do people give you the gift of: communication; family; self-disclosure (communicating information about yourself); wisdom; appreciation; listening; asking questions; encouragement; patience; affirmation; knowledge; friendship; Self-Esteem; T.U.A. (Total Unconditional Acceptance); love; forgiveness; freedom from guilt, blame and value judgment; being present to you; play; fun and laughter; inclusion; kindness; compassion; tears; being sensitive; being child-like; health; your career; or the gift of celebrating Thanksgiving?

You may want to do something special for another person outside your family. Look around. Who can you serve? Learn to create "magic" moments for people. How can you give yourself away to make someone's life better this Thanksgiving or in general?

Take action now **and then, watch what happens!**

> *"I now appreciate all of my skills*
> *and gifts daily."*

Are You Interested In A Quantum Leap?

What do you remember most about the past 12 months? Do you have a checklist of what you accomplished?

Review the list below and respond to each by asking, "Do I appreciate myself for":

1. Taking care of my health?
2. Going to work every day and for being on time?
3. Learning new skills?
4. My patience?
5. Helping others become more competent?
6. My creativity?
7. Upgrading my attitudes?
8. Improving my listening skills?

9. Learning the Art of Asking Questions?
10. Reading more books?
11. Listening to self-development tapes?
12. Attending seminars and other learning experiences?
13. Balancing my left and right brain?
14. Taking vacations?
15. Exercising daily?
16. Helping people *feel* better about themselves?
17. Reading one new person a day? (Asking a person questions for the purpose of getting to know them.)
18. Encouraging people to BE themselves?
19. Planning my future?
20. Accepting responsibility for everything I think, say, do and *feel?*
21. Appreciating my parents?
22. Sending thank-you notes to people?
23. Improving customer/client services?
24. Developing my Self-Esteem?

You may want to write in your daily journal and recall all the things you appreciate about yourself and the choices you have made in the past 12 months.

As you look to the future, and especially next year, what do you want to look back on at this time next year? What skills do you want to learn? How much money do you want to earn? What value system will you choose? What does fulfillment mean to you? Will you develop a mentor relationship with someone who will help you take a quantum leap with your life?

I wish you health and prosperity on your journey to intact Self-Esteem and fulfillment.

Now is the time to appreciate your past and prepare for the future **and then, watch what happens!**

> *"I now appreciate my past and prepare to take a quantum leap in the next year."*

What Outcomes Do You Want 10 Years From Now?

How would you evaluate the past ten years of your life? What were the highlights of your life for this decade? What did you do with your time? Did you spend it or invest it? What is your definition of success?

Alex Mackenzie has studied how people use their time. His definition of success is, "Doing your best." I believe most people want to make the most out of themselves. Almost all successful people attribute their success to setting and achieving goals. I'm suggesting you look at the outcomes you obtained. We all receive outcomes in our life, although we may not achieve all of our goals. When you look at the outcomes you obtained, I believe it teaches you more about you.

As you review the past ten years, what outcomes did you receive? You are now 10 years older. How many times have you said any of the following?

- "I've always dreamed of...."
- "I wish I could...."
- "Someday I'm going to...."
- "Next year I'm really going to...."

As you look back over the past ten years, did you achieve the outcomes you wanted? What lessons have you learned in the past decade? Are you interested in preparing for the future? Here are some questions to serve you in knowing the outcomes you want in the next ten years.

1. What is most important in your personal and work life?
2. What percentage of your time will you devote to each area of your life?
3. What standard of health do you want to achieve or maintain?
4. How can your personal relationships be improved?
5. What new skills will you learn?
6. How much money do you want to earn?
7. What is your ultimate ideal career? Do you want to change your job, career or business?

8. What books will you read?
9. Who will mentor you to guide you to take quantum leaps in the next 10 years? I encourage you to have at least one mentor in each area of your life.
10. How will you know you have obtained your outcomes?
11. What will accomplishing the outcomes do for you?

Remember, as you work toward your outcomes, you may have some detours. When this happens, just ask yourself what skills you need to acquire to obtain the outcomes you want. It is also acceptable to upgrade and refine your outcomes along the way. Outcomes are not set in marble. As you develop, you may have new insights and acquire new skills and knowledge that causes you to adjust the outcomes you want. Be gentle with yourself. This may be new territory.

Take a few minutes now to write down the outcomes you want in the next 10 years **and then, watch what happens!**

> *"I now write down the outcomes I want during the next 10 years."*

What Light Is In Your Life?

Do you remember the song, *You Light Up My Life?* Do you recall when President Bush was elected? He talked about 1,000 points of light. During the November, December and January holiday season do you go to see the colorful lights in different parts of your city? At the beginning of each new decade focus on the word—*LIGHT.*

Pause for a moment and review the past 10 years. How did you light up your life? Did you have a mentor—a resource person (or persons) who helped you improve your life in all areas: Spiritual, Financial, Social, Mental, Physical, Family and Career? I believe every person needs to find at least one mentor who is interested in helping them release more of their potential.

Each decade offers its own challenges.
1. Meaningful relationships
2. All kinds of addictions and their consequences
3. Career transitions and uncertainty about the future
4. Health care
5. Aging and the possibility of living beyond 100
6. Financial planning and answering the question, "How much money will I need to live a dignified retirement lifestyle?"

Here are some ideas for your planning of the next 10 years of your life, using the acrostic *LIGHT.*

L—Lifelong Learning. Do you have a *Lifelong Learning Program?*

I—Investing. Are you *investing* money for your retirement? Do you invest in yourself daily by refining and learning new skills? No one is as interested in you as you are!

G—Go! Where will you *go* in the next 10 years to visit new places, meet new people and broaden your life experiences?

H—Health. What *health* improvements will you make daily?

T—Time. How will you use your *time* in the next 10 years? That's 3650 days! Will you spend them or invest them?

Whatever you decide to do, let your *light* shine daily during the next 10 years to give and receive the most out of your life. Remember these words Lifelong Learning, Invest, Go, Health, and Time. I wish you a healthy and prosperous decade.

Find the mentors to help you get the most from your life **and then, watch what happens!**

"I now light up my life daily by having and being a mentor."

Are You Happy Giving and Receiving?

What is the holiday season all about? Is it about receiving presents or is it about giving presents? Are you happiest when you are giving or receiving? What was your greatest gift to another person? What was the greatest gift you ever received? Do you still have that gift?

Each time you answered the above questions, you experienced some *feelings*. Many people have difficulty describing their *feelings*. Often they are afraid to be honest about their *feelings* because it makes them uncomfortable. *Feelings* are neither good or bad. They just "are." During the holiday season we are exposed to all kinds of *feelings*. Some of those *feelings* are sadness, loneliness, happiness and love.

Mary Tenoever, a graduate of our Self-Esteem Program, told me about a children's book called *Feelings* by Barbara Kay Polland. There are pictures of a frustrated child, a happy baby, a frightened little girl and many others. Let's look at the *feelings* of sadness. When do you *feel* sad? How do you show that you *feel* sad? Do people close to you *feel* sad? As you read the following words, how do you feel?

Downcast

Glum

Grieved

Dejected

Depressed

Look in a mirror. Does your face show sadness? How do you release sadness?

Another *feeling* during the holiday season is loneliness. Do you ever *feel* lonely? Are you lonely when you are by yourself? Are you ever lonely at a party or in crowded places? Can you describe *feelings* of loneliness? Depression, fright, shyness, boredom and withdrawal are words identified with loneliness. What do you do to stop *feeling* lonely?

Now, what about the *feeling* of happiness? Complete these sentences.

1. I am happy when....
2. I show my happiness by....

3. Other people are happy when....
4. My happiest moments are....
5. The happiest person I know is....

Look at yourself in the mirror. Smile and look and feel happy.

Finally, how do you identify the *feeling* of love? Complete these sentences.

1. I love it when I....
2. I love it when people....
3. I show my love for people when....
4. I describe love as....

My definition of love is T.U.A. (Total Unconditional Acceptance).

As you experience the holiday season and other times of the year, invest in *feelings* of T.U.A. for yourself and everyone you meet. Start a *feelings* journal now and begin describing your *feelings* daily **and then, watch what happens!**

> *"I now create happiness by giving T.U.A. to myself and others."*

Do You Write In A Journal?

Happy New You!! Did you write down the outcomes your wanted for the past year? Did you make New Year's resolutions for the past and upcoming year? How many did you keep? How many will you keep?

A few years ago I asked my nephew, Bill Winters, about what the new year meant to him. He said, "I believe it means opportunity." We have new opportunities to progress towards new outcomes.

Mel Tillis, the Country and Western singer, said, "I stuttered and was ridiculed as a child. However, my mother told me I could do anything. Just keep moving forward every day toward what you want." He still stutters. Yet, he has impacted millions of people with his music. He is a role model for those who need to transcend speech impediments. His vision and commitment created a burning desire for total use of his talent.

A piece of mail once came to my home reading, "You Have Inherited OVER 1/2 Million! In fact your inheritance averages out to be 573,450—no, not in money. It is in something more important—TIME!" It said, "The average person lives 573,450 hours." Then it said, "Your hours are running out and so are mine."

Yes, we all have needs, wants and values. We all have 24 hours a day for the rest of our lives to achieve our outcomes. It's what we do with time that determines our outcomes. Decide now to do something specific everyday in the 7 areas of your life: Spiritual, Social, Mental, Physical, Financial, Career and Family. Write down in your journal what you want to BE, do and have.

Many people allow life to run them. If you identify with this, begin now to run your own life. Every night spend a few minutes writing in a journal. When you take the time to write out and focus on the outcomes you want, then you are taking the first steps to creating your life the way you want it. Make notes of what you did, what you learned and the outcomes you received each day.

"Plus" (add to) your life by listening to educational audiocassette tapes and reading at least one self-development book every month. In order to become an expert in any field, you need to read 20 minutes a day, for 6 months. Decide to refine one skill each year. Find mentors to help you obtain the outcomes you want.

Tell no one of the outcomes you want except your mentors **and then, watch what happens!**

"I now write in my journal daily."

Are You Environmentally Conscious?

What does the holiday season mean to you? For many people it simply means the end of the year. Some people *feel* it is a time of loneliness. For other people, it means anticipation of a new year, a new beginning.

What choices have you made between Thanksgiving and New Year's Day? Are you unhappy and lonely or are you excited and fulfilled? What makes the difference?

Based on my 40 years of qualitative research in Self-Esteem, I believe all unhappiness and violence is a request for love. As you may recall, my definition for love is T.U.A. (Total Unconditional Acceptance).

During the holiday season, our Self-Esteem is tested every day by the people we meet and the activities we choose. This is a season when we are often involved with more people. Ask yourself what would need to exist for you to:

1. Listen more when people are speaking?
2. Avoid finishing someone's sentence?
3. Avoid anticipating what someone will say?
4. Decide to give people eye contact?
5. Give people your undivided attention and focus on them exclusively?
6. Ask questions?
7. Release playing games of one-upmanship and comparison?

The above are examples of intact Self-Esteem behavior. Do any of these suggestions cost money? No! Will you receive an Academy Award for that behavior? No! Will people thank you for your intact Self-Esteem and sensitivity? Could be. Will you *feel* better about yourself? Yes!! Will you want to affirm people more and more? Yes!

As you decide to practice staying away from toxic environments, you will be associating more frequently with people who like themselves. People always show how they *feel* about themselves (Self-Esteem) by the way they treat you. With intact Self-Esteem, happiness and success are inevitable. Happy Holidays! Happy New Year! Happy New You!

Decide to make a New Year's resolution to create a prosperous intact Self-Esteem affirming environment wherever you go **and then, watch what happens!**

> *"I now create a prosperous intact Self-Esteem affirming environment."*

How Appreciative Are You?

What do the holidays mean to you? Are you looking forward to the free time? Is being together with your family important? Will you attend year-end parties with your family and friends? Will it be a time when you evaluate your choices and your achievements? Will you be concerned with transitions in your relationships and career? Will you invest a few moments to review if and how your Self-Esteem has improved during the past year? Will you be convinced that you never take a vacation from your Self-Esteem?

Remember, Self-Esteem is the self-respect you *feel* for yourself. The holiday season, like all others, is a time to do some self-appreciation. Congratulate yourself for taking care of yourself, your family, your career and your friendships.

Add up all the moments you *gave yourself away* to help someone. Add up all of the smiles you gave away and then received a smile in return. Recall all the times you gave someone a firm handshake. Remember how you *felt* when someone said "thank you" for your opening a door or holding open a door for them. Reflect on the times you gave information to your fellow employees or associates to help make their work easier. Appreciate the quiet moments you gave yourself. Recall relaxing to your favorite mellow music. Relish those vacation memories when you renewed your desire to experience life at a cutting edge level. Take delight in those experiences which helped you *feel* alive. Relive those special moments when you went to your favorite restaurant and enjoyed conversation at the highest plateau (the highest form of conversation, free of value judging, gossip and envy).

Close your eyes and see all of those precious moments of the past year. Hear the beautiful sounds and *feel* the unique *feelings* of intact Self-Esteem which you deserve.

I appreciate you reading this message. We all need to love each other to bring about peace on earth. With intact Self-Esteem, peace, happiness and success are inevitable. I wish you and your loved ones health, wealth and to always be young among old friends. And I wish you and your loved ones intact Self-Esteem.

Share this message with others **and then, watch what happens!**

> *"I now appreciate and love myself because I exist!"*

Chapter Six

Lifestyle

What Is Your Strategy For Living?

Do you have a strategy for daily living? Do you have a set of guidelines to follow to direct your life to reach your fullest potential? Only you can decide what you need, want and value. A strategy is planning, directing and adjusting to the outcomes you need, want and value. You live your plan one day at a time. Dr. Ari Kiev wrote a book, *A Strategy for Living.* I was reviewing it and thought I would share some of his ideas with you.

All of us have developed habits that move us backward or forward. Just as we cannot take a vacation from our Self-Esteem, we cannot release old habits until we find a replacement. When I stopped drinking coffee, I replaced it with hot chocolate. As I became aware that hot chocolate was adding pounds to my body, I found herbal tea as a replacement. I had a plan and a direction; however, I needed to adjust to obtain the best outcomes. Once you know what your dreams and the outcomes you want are, then you can design your daily strategy.

The five enemies that prevents us from success are: greed, ambition, envy, anger and pride. Dr. Kiev suggests eight strategies for your consideration.

1. Decide on a purpose. A powerful dream creates a dynamic force within you. Anyone who fixes on a purpose and pursues it can be successful.
2. Discover your hidden potential. Every person has a Unique Factor. Find out what it is and develop it.
3. What outcomes will you select daily? Are you a self-starter regardless of the circumstances?
4. Do you have a step-by-step plan? Do you use your time wisely? Make a list of your daily activities. Then observe if you are spending or investing your time.
5. What behavior will you be changing? Do you want to stop smoking, lose weight and/or be more affirming? Are you afraid of changing any behavior that is holding you back?
6. Are you financially self-reliant? Is your standard of living and lifestyle acceptable to you? Are you on target with your financial outcomes?

7. Do you depend on others for your *feelings* about your self or are you self-sufficient? Are you a "people pleaser" or do you respect yourself by taking charge of your own life and making your own decisions?

8. Do you invest a portion of your day in service to others? People with intact Self-Esteem focus on others. How are you giving yourself away every day?

Design your daily strategy for living **and then, watch what happens!**

> *"I now focus on a daily strategy for living."*

How Easy Is Decision Making?

Is it generally easy for you to make decisions? Are you afraid of decision making mistakes? What made you decide to read this book? When did you learn to make your own decisions? Did your parents make decisions for you and were you stuck with the consequences? How did you make decisions about your: learning experiences, spirituality, career, skills, friends, residence, food, marital status, financial plan, child rearing and restoring your intact Self-Esteem? How do you decide what to do every day?

Here are some ideas for you to consider as you choose what to decide each day. Many people analyze the situation when they are uncertain what to do. If you analyze, you can stay stuck in analysis and never take action. *The secret of decision making success is intuition!*

Intuition is the act or process of coming to direct knowledge or certainty without reasoning or rational thought. It is revelation by insight or innate knowledge. Intuition is the direct perception of truth, immediate apprehension and understanding. It is independent of any reasoning process. You need to "feel" a decision, to move from reliance on logic to an acceptance of intuition. The intuitive approach is often the most creative and reliable when you seek solutions to challenges.

Here are four steps that can help you with the decision making process.

1. Total immersion. Collect all the information. Talk to all the people involved. Avoid coming to any conclusions or any answers.

2. Incubation. Step back, pause and stop collecting details. Let the information incubate. Let your intuition process the information.

3. Eureka moment. This is the "Aha" moment when insight is acquired and you make a decision. This usually occurs during a moment of relaxation.

4. Verification. This last step is when logic and evaluation are especially important. Unfortunately, many people ignore it. Before you make the decision, evaluate the consequences, the price you will pay and all the implications.

So relax, make your own decisions **and then, watch what happens!**

> *"I now make my own decisions since I have to live with the consequences."*

How Are Your Questioning Skills?

Have you heard the name Socrates? He left us a special gift, a legacy forever. He is my hero, my mentor! He knew the power of asking questions. He gave us two powerful words— "Know Thyself."

Many people are afraid to know themselves. They live their lives externally. People with intact Self-Esteem love internally and are constantly open to learn more about themselves. They recognize that the more they know about themselves, the more they understand and are willing to learn about others. Their world is constantly expanding and they love meeting people. They often use actor and humorist Will Rogers' comment, "I never meet a stranger."

Here is where Socrates' teachings can contribute to your learning. You can teach and learn in three ways: telling, coaching or by use of the Socratic method of asking questions. I call this system of asking questions, "discovery learning." Socrates was a wordsmith. He valued words and ideas. He was also concerned about how a person's mind works. His method was qualitative. That is, he used the Art of Asking Questions. By asking questions, he could obtain clarity and definitions of the words people used, rather than depending solely on his perception of what was being communicated. Perceptions can be incorrect. Socrates' power has lasted for thousands of years. How many of our words or ideas last for more than a few seconds or minutes?

If you observe people's behavior, you can be aware of their needs. People's values can be recognized by the words they choose. Words are powerful! Words create *feelings*, and Self-Esteem is a *feeling*.

I believe *the key to success with people is "curiosity."* First, you need to be curious about your own thoughts and *feelings*. You need to ask yourself questions to get to know yourself, in-depth. You can also choose to be curious about others and discover their thoughts and *feelings* through the Art of Asking Questions. As you look to your future, consider evaluating your words, how you "language" those words, and the Art of Asking Questions. Words are the tools used in our society to communicate. When you refine these tools, you can have better understanding and more in-depth communication with each person you meet.

Socrates said, "My mother was a midwife and I followed in my mother's footsteps." Socrates was a mental obstetrician. He helped people give birth to their ideas.

In the next twelve months develop the skills of Socrates. Help yourself and others give birth to dormant ideas **and then, watch what happens!**

> *"I now develop Socrates' skills by learning the Art of Asking Questions."*

What Are Your Priorities?

Do you ever wish you had more time? Everyone has 24 hours a day. No one has any "spare" time and no one "wastes" time. You either spend your time or invest your time. Some health authorities suggest we sleep eight hours. Most people work eight hours a day. That leaves eight hours a day, plus Saturday, Sunday and vacation time to do whatever we need, want and value.

Research shows that Americans spent 17 hours a week watching television, 7.9 hours eating, 5.7 hours shopping, 4.5 hours cooking, 2.9 hours exercising or recreating, 2.8 hours housecleaning, 1.9 hours in church and civic work, 0.7 gardening and pet care. How do you *feel* about this research? Do you *feel* you need more time? If you had more time, how would you invest it? Would you invest it in your: career, fun, travel, learning, social experiences, family, relationships and something else? Where are the pressures in your life? What are you doing about these pressures?

Here are some questions to help you evaluate your time.

1. Are you the master of your time or are you a slave to time?
2. Do you manage your schedule so that you do not need to rush?
3. Are you equally prompt with your: management, peers, business associates, family, friends, etc.?
4. Do you set your watch ahead in order to be prompt for appointments?
5. When you are given an assignment, is it completed on schedule, late or ahead of schedule?
6. When you are hired to do a job, do you give it your all?
7. Do you avoid cutting corners and give as much as promised, or even more?
8. Do you accept each assignment or opportunity as a fresh challenge and a chance to develop in your career and as a person?
9. Are you well balanced in the seven areas of life: Mental, Spiritual, Physical, Social, Financial, Career and Family?

People with intact Self-Esteem have completion in their lives because they finish what they begin. Be sure to think carefully before you take on any task. Once you start it—complete it with thoroughness, energy and resolve.

Learn to say "no" to any invitation that differs from your priorities **and then, watch what happens!**

> *"I now invest my time in my priorities."*

How Do You Use Your Time?

Do you know what you are looking for? Will you know it when you see, hear and *feel* it? We all have 365 days a year, 24 hours a day and 60 minutes an hour. What causes some people to accomplish hundreds of complex tasks while other people lay buried under a sea of papers and challenges and seem to be going nowhere?

How do you use the time available to you? Your answers determine many vital things about your life, such as:

1. What priorities you get done at work.
2. How much time you can visit with people.
3. How you create your life the way you want it.
4. Whether you *feel* a sense of moving backward, forward or of standing still.
5. How you *feel* about yourself? I call that your Self-Esteem.

The way you use your time affects your moods and helps determine whether you *feel* stressed or relaxed. The way you use your time determines whether you *feel* that you are running your life or it is running you. Effective use of your time requires skill. It is a Self-Esteem issue.

Would you like to make your life simpler and more fun? The first step is to ask yourself this question several times a day: "What is the best use of my time right now?"

Here are some key concepts about how to invest your time for the best results.

1. Write down the outcomes you want for the day, week, year, 5 years, 10 years and 15 years from now. The outcomes you need, want and value will indicate the general direction of your life.
2. Establish objectives. Clarify the direction of your life.
3. Set priorities. Make an A (#1 priority), B (#2 priority), and C (#3 priority) list. Always focus immediately on the A list.
4. Evaluate your time use. Schedule your important tasks during your most productive hours. Avoid unwise use of time such as interruptions, getting ready to get ready, casual conversations and anything that takes you away from "the best use of your time now!"
5. Every week make a plan for yourself, including scheduling free time. You deserve nurturing and pampering!
6. Put first things first. Decide what is important today and do something about it today. Put unimportant things on the bottom of the pile.
7. Relax! Reward yourself every day.

Celebrate your successes and accomplishments daily **and then, watch what happens!**

> *"I now ask myself, 'What is the best use of my time now?'"*

How Can You Survive And Thrive?

What is the best thing that happened to you in the past six months? What did you want in the past six months? Did you accomplish what you wanted? Do you want friends? How do you get them and keep them? Do you want more fun? Just what does fun mean to you? Do you want less distress? What is your first step to release the pressure? Do you want more money? How will you obtain it? What will you do with it? What do you want to buy? Do you want a vacation? Where would you go? Are you fulfilled in your career? What will you be planning for the 21st Century? What have you learned in the past six months? What new skills will help you become more competent? How will you motivate yourself to guarantee that you will have sustained interest to acquire the success you want?

Just what is the secret of success? Do you believe it is complicated or simple? How do you *feel* about this next idea about success? Here it is—*Giving is the secret of creating success.* The meaning of success is still the same. Our society needs to acquire a whole new way of thinking, doing and being. Giving of ourselves helps us to *feel* more successful in our work lives as well as our personal lives. That is what success is all about for now and the future.

Now is the time to prepare for the new skills you will need to survive and thrive. Do you know that success is magnetic? Your Self-Esteem is the magnet. Unintact Self-Esteem repels. Intact Self-Esteem attracts. Comparing yourself to others destroys your Self-Esteem. Helping and serving others builds your Self-Esteem.

Ralph Waldo Emerson defined success like this:

> *To laugh often and much; to win the respect of intelligent people and the affection of children; to earn the appreciation of honest critics and endure the betrayal of false friends; to appreciate beauty; to find the best in others; to leave the world a bit better whether by a healthy child, a garden patch or a redeemed social condition; to know even one life has breathed easier because you have lived. This is to have succeeded.*

This is an excellent definition of success. Will you have the sustained interest necessary to believe in yourself? Will you find mentors to help you get where you want to go? Will you find a cause that is bigger than life and invest your energy to create harmony and peace in the world?

Here are eight suggestions to move you toward your outcomes.

1. Identify your skills.
2. Become a better observer of what is happening in the world.

3. Take action by releasing old goals and creating the outcomes you want.
4. Keep a success journal.
5. Practice giving and receiving compliments, which are gifts. "Thank You" is the best way to accept a compliment.
6. Practice deliberate, intelligent behavior.
7. Laugh daily.
8. Work on your Self-Esteem daily.

Give something back daily **and then, watch what happens!"**

> *"I choose to give to others to help them survive and thrive."*

What Is A Summer Review?

Have you heard the song, *Summertime and the Living Is Easy?* How is the summer (or how was last summer) for you? Are you relaxing? Are you returning from or going on a vacation? Are you planning or doing new things? Are you experiencing more of life? Are you meeting new people? Are you reading more books? Are you listening to more personal and professional development audiocassette tapes? Are you developing your people skills?

Are you an interesting person to listen to? Are you showing interest in others by asking them questions about what interests them? Do you give specific feedback to people to affirm their ideas and competence? Do you stay in touch with friends to let them know how important their friendship is to you? Do you upgrade your career skills daily so that you maximize your potential? Are you where you want to be with your career? What is the state of your physical and mental health?

Do you have a mentor(s)—someone to guide you and help you get where you want to go? Do you have any children or do you come in contact with children? Do you treat them with dignity and respect? Have you observed any children

12 years old or older? Are you interested in having their Self-Esteem be more intact? Would you be interested in a classic book that can help young people's Self-Esteem? Would you give at least one young person the book *I Dare You* and encourage them to read the book? Or you could *choose to give it to a group or classroom of young people.*

Now is the time to prepare for the future. Business and organizational work places will constantly demand competence and people skills. We need to put together an American style apprentice system that provides specific training for all people. The bottom line for all of this is intact Self-Esteem. Young people need to have role models that will show them how to be prepared for life. They need to develop their talents. They need to have the skills to be flexible enough to handle the "what ifs" that emerge along life's path. "What if" I: get fired, am successful or unsuccessful, become ill, need more skills or have to be reeducated? Young people need you to model an affirming lifestyle.

Your Self-Esteem determines your interest, involvement and commitment in developing your skills to their fullest potential. Remember, with intact Self-Esteem, happiness and success is inevitable.

Enjoy the summer, prepare for your future daily, let a youngster be an apprentice to you **and then, watch what happens!**

> *"I now create an affirming*
> *Self-Esteem lifestyle."*

Do You Spring Clean?

Have you done your spring cleaning yet? Do you *feel* it is important for you to review where you have been, where you are now and where you are going? Are your plans set for the rest of the year? What is working in your life? What needs to be refined? Do you review your attitudes to see the way you think? Have you been checking up on your Self-Esteem?

Spring is a time to clean out, spruce up and experience the budding of new things. What newness will you be adding to your life? What do you really, really, really, really, really, really, really want? How will you get what you want? *One of the ways to acquire what you really want is to "affirm" what you want and then act on it.* This affirmation system can help you obtain whatever you want in life.

There are three requirements to this affirmation system. You need to:

1. Write down the outcomes you want. Make sure you work through any unaffirming (negative) *feelings.* This can be done by noticing the unaffirming *feelings,* accepting them and letting them go by saying "cancel, cancel."
2. Say your affirmations out loud, with *feeling,* at least three times a day.
3. "Act on" your affirmations. If you want something you need to take action to acquire the outcomes.

Here are some affirmations to consider for your spring cleaning. Repeat these several times a day.

1. I welcome this new day.
2. I now have a fresh start.
3. I now choose to begin anew, letting go of unhealthy thoughts, *feelings* and attitudes that stifle my development.
4. I now *feel* free to move on to healthier ideas, thoughts and emotions.
5. I now take steps toward attaining my outcomes.
6. I now clarify my values and live according to them.
7. I now listen attentively to all those with whom I come in contact.
8. I am now calm and relaxed.
9. I now make excellent decisions.
10. I now improve my Self-Esteem.

You can obtain the outcomes you want when you say and take action on your affirmations **and then, watch what happens!**

> **"I do spring cleaning to prepare
> for the rest of the year."**

What Is Your Life Plan?

Do you have a life plan? Do you review it every day? Does your plan include the seven areas of life, which are: Spiritual, Mental, Financial, Social, Physical, Family and Career? Are you acting every day on your plan?

First, may I suggest you write a life inventory. Write down your values as well as all of the things you do and would like to do. Here are eight categories for you to consider.

1. List the peak experiences you have had. Psychologist Abraham Maslow described peak experiences as "the most ecstatic, euphoric and most pleasant experiences of your life." I believe the more intact your Self-Esteem is, the more peak experiences you will have. Some people use drugs or alcohol to get an instant rush of euphoria. The major difference is that it is a temporary high. It always ends! A peak experience releases the ever-present drug in your brain called endorphins. When our endorphins are flowing, we have a *feeling* of well-being and wholeness. This can happen when we see a beautiful sunset or hear our favorite music. Plan daily for more peak experiences by refining your Self-Esteem.

2. List all the things you do well.

3. List all the things you do not do well. Put them all on paper for you to see.

4. What are the things you would like to stop doing? Would you like to stop smoking, lose weight, drink less alcohol? Write them down.

5. What are the things you would like to learn to do well? Develop new skills daily.

6. What values do you want to live by? Take a moment now to write down your most cherished values. They could include family, love, health, religion, money and friends. You decide.

7. List the peak experiences you plan to have in the future.

8. List the things you would like to start doing now.

Review these eight categories daily. Develop and act on your life plan **and then, watch what happens!**

> *"I now develop and act on*
> *my life plan daily."*

Are You In Charge Of Your Life?

Are you in charge of your life? Have you taken effective charge of your life with intact Self-Esteem? The only way to know is to look at the outcomes you are receiving in your life. Listen to the feedback you receive from yourself and others. Experience your *feelings* concerning the respect you *feel* for yourself.

To take charge of your life the intact Self-Esteem way, ask yourself these questions.

1. What do I need, want and value?

2. What would be a demonstration of these needs,wants and values?

3. How would I know if I had what I needed, wanted and valued?

4. When do I need, want and value them?

5. What would happen if I received them?

6. What stops me from having them?

7. When do I not need, want and value them?

When you answer these questions, you can evaluate how you have taken charge of your life. Review the seven areas of your life: Spiritual, Mental, Physical, Social, Financial, Career and Family. What outcomes have you obtained in each of these areas that convinces you that you are moving in the direction you want to go? Do you need to change directions in any of these areas? If so, how? Your Self-Esteem determines the clarity of your value system. When your values are clear, decision making is easy. When your Self-Esteem is intact, happiness and success are inevitable.

As you evaluate your needs, wants and values, you may see pictures, hear sounds or sense that you are on target. These pictures, sounds or what you sense indicates how satisfied you are with your life. Your life is a series of choices. You have a choice to have unintact or intact Self-Esteem. You are either controlled by external events and others or you are taking charge of your life by being inner-directed. Being inner-directed helps you to take charge of your life the Self-Esteem way.

Be inner-directed by taking action with the easiest next step. Reread your review of the seven areas of your life. Of all the things you need, want and value, which is the easiest next step that is guaranteed to work? Do it now and then proceed to the second easiest next step.

When you do this, you can gradually take charge of your life and receive the outcomes you need, want, and value in all areas of your life **and then, watch what happens!"**

> *"I now take charge of my life*
> *the Self-Esteem way."*

Would You Like Harmonious Relationships?

Have you ever wanted to change any of your behaviors? Did you ever want to change your job or career? Would you like to change your eating or drinking habits? Did you ever want to change your communication skills? Do you want to upgrade your speaking, writing or listening skills? If you are a teacher, do you use all three teaching skills: didactic (telling), coaching or the Socratic method, which is the Art of Asking Questions?

Research shows that discovery learning is the best way to learn anything. In 1967, I made a major change in my communication skills by learning to externally listen. My relationships with others immediately became more harmonious. Prior to that I talked too much and rarely heard what was being said because I was so concerned about what I would say next. I used to have constant internal dialogue. The change took place when I realized my lack of skills was a Self-Esteem issue.

As I improved my Self-Esteem, I respected myself more and my relationships improved. The more intact my Self-Esteem, the more secure I was a person and the greater value I gave to other people. It was easier to work with people and appreciate their points of view. I learned to negotiate and compromise without giving up my values. I stopped criticizing people who had different opinions. I asked more questions to clarify issues so there would be mutually beneficial outcomes.

Self-Esteem is an essential ingredient in changing your behavior, and it is needed to create harmony, cooperation and trust. Do you see yourself as a change agent? Are you open to new ideas that you can make a significant impact on the relationships you have with your family, students, employees, business associates or community?

Everyone is a role model with his or her behavior. When you change your behavior, other people are more likely to learn and may be open to change. The question is, "Are you modeling intact Self-Esteem behavior?" Here are some ideas to consider as you change your behavior to create harmonious relationships.

1. Evaluate your communication skills. Do you give people your undivided attention? Do you wait for people to finish their sentences? Do you ask questions to learn more about them?
2. Do you hear what people say, clarify if necessary and give them feedback about what you heard?
3. Do you affirm others? You can only affirm people up to the level that you have been affirmed.
4. Do you act natural with people so that they know you are genuine and real?

5. Are you willing to grow and develop mutually beneficial relationships?
6. Will you educate yourself to work on your Self-Esteem daily?

If you want to be a change agent, first change yourself **and then, watch what happens!**

> *"I now create harmonious relationships by changing my behavior."*

What Is Success?

Are you ready for the future? How are you doing with your plans for the future? Have you worked on looking at the outcomes you want in the future? What is your definition for success? What is your success system? Have you begun a Lifelong Learning Program? How are you focusing on creating balance in all seven areas of your life?

Every day it is important to focus some time on each area: Spiritual, Mental, Social, Physical, Financial, Career and Family. The key word here is *focus*. Ideas abound everywhere. It is the ideas we focus and take action on that make the difference.

My definition of success is having intact Self-Esteem every day. What is your definition? Here are some ideas for success.

1. Answer the question, "What do you really, really, really, really, really, really, really want?"
2. Write out a 1 year, 5 year and 10 year plan to project what you want to BE, do and have.
3. Take advantage of the many sources of expertise and learning.
4. Establish a relationship with mentors who can give you direction in the seven areas of your life.
5. Learn from courses, seminars, books and audio cassettes.

Success often takes more than talent. I suggest you work smarter not harder. You need to know how to seize the moment. The key to success is inner excitement, direction and challenge. This is the reason successful people are invariably more interesting to be around throughout their entire lives.

When you seek your own definition of success, you can be more alive than those who do not. You can be more observant and focus on and take the necessary action. You will more likely be inner-directed rather then outer-directed. As a result, you are more likely to be values-driven. You will be more aware of how to create and have satisfaction, fulfillment and peace of mind. You will be better able to adjust to set backs, correct for error and move forward in an affirming, intact Self-Esteem manner.

Learn to notice, focus and act on that which will serve you in obtaining the success you want **and then, watch what happens!**

> *"I now focus on success by being inner-directed."*

What Is Your Level Of Success?

What does success really mean to you? Is money success? Is power success? Is having your own business success? Is competence success? Is freedom success? Is having friends success? Is health success? Is being in love success? Is being single or married success? Is having a family success? Is having possessions success? Is self acceptance success? Is Self-Esteem behavior success?

My wife Dean and I once attended a play called, *Have*. It was about women who wanted to "Have" property and land. The play centered on how they went about acquiring these items. Their acquisitions meant success to them.

All of us choose our own success. Give yourself a success checkup. Do you consider yourself energetic? Do you think you have what it really takes to succeed? Are you willing to learn and take the necessary action to be successful? What, if anything, are you willing to give up in order to succeed? Do you think women are as ambitious as men? Answer these questions and the ones below.

1. What is your work style: hard driving, high pressure, relaxed or just to get the job done?
2. How many hours a week do you work?
3. What are your priorities in life? Is it becoming financially well-off, having a great family life, living a creative life, making a contribution to society, developing rewarding personal relationships, achieving recognition, improving your skills, achieving job or career success or enhancing your Self-Esteem?
4. Regardless of how you *feel* about your work, how successful do you *feel* you are with your: career, talent, abilities, risk-taking, hard work, determination, education, family role and relationships, perseverance, need to succeed, personality, high standards, personal or family wealth and personal fulfillment?
5. Which do you *feel* is more important for achieving excellence in your work: competition or cooperation? How come?

When you BE and then do and have with intact Self-Esteem, happiness and success are inevitable **and then, watch what happens!**

> *"I now choose to build my Self-Esteem to achieve my highest level of success."*

How Do You Create Your Future?

Are you aware that George Burns, the comedy king, will be 100 years old in 1996? He is in great demand to share his sense of humor all over the world. In fact the Paladium in London, England has booked him and is sold out for his 100th birthday performance. George intends to keep that engagement. His trademarks are his cigar, his one liners, his perfect timing and his unique singing style.

How has George made it this far? He said his sustaining energy comes from his audiences. He fell in love with show business when he was eight years old. It took him 20 years to get recognized and become an "overnight success." When asked, "What is your secret for success?" he said, "Fall in love with you "future"! What a great idea. Our future is in the next moment. The future is now. What you do now and in the next moment determines the direction of your life. Let's take a look at the word "future" as an acrostic.

F – Fun. Do you want to make your future *fun?* When you laugh and have fun you release pure endorphins from your brain. This creates a *feeling* of euphoria. Research shows that distress destroys energy and creates the possibility of sickness. George Burns believes in growing old playfully.

U – Unique Factor. Have you discovered your *"unique factor"*—your special talent?

T – Time. It takes *time* to reach age 100 and to reach your full potential. Research also shows it takes fifteen years, on the average, to become an "overnight success"!

U – Update. *Update* your future, moment-to-moment. By living in the moment, the future becomes more exciting because the future is now in the next moment.

R – Responsibility. When we accept *responsibility* for everything we think, say, do and *feel*, our future is built on a solid foundation.

E – Esteem. Your *Esteem* is the self respect you *feel* for yourself. A healthy and happy future depends on your Self-Esteem.

George Burns reached his age because he enjoys the present and he fell in love with his future. He was flexible enough to adjust to all the changes that occurred in his life. Determine what needs to exist for you to listen to his suggestion. Live in the present moment, fall in love with your future **and then, watch what happens!"**

> *"I now fall in love with my future."*

What Is Your Favorite Quote?

Do you like quotations? Here are some quotations of wisdom from famous people. You may want to write some of your favorites in your journal for future reference.

"For every minute you are angry you lose 60 seconds of happiness." —Ralph Waldo Emerson

"Love is nature's second sun causing a spring of virtues when he shines." —George Chapman

"Think of people as adventures." —Lawrence Durrell

"There is no learning to live without learning to love." —Father John Powell

"Ask yourself how come you are so much more aware of the irritating qualities of other people rather than their fine qualities? Common sense is only wisdom applied to conduct." —William James

"Culture is acquainting ourselves with the best that has ever been known and said in the world." —Matthew Arnold

"He who is hurried cannot walk gracefully." —Old Chinese Proverb

"No new truth is ever really learned until it is acted upon." —Father John Powell

"No nation has ever been involved in war solely because its inhabitants excelled in creating great poetry, music, or painting. And when all the clocks and calendars have stopped their counting for you, what then has your life added up to? There are two creatures in nature that exhibit impatience— men and puppies. There is one thing you can depend on; people who are interested in power are not interested in people." —John Ward

"Nothing is so vulgar as to be in a hurry." —Oliver Wendell Holmes

"When people have killed joy—I do not believe they still live. The only love that counts for anything is that which reveals itself not in deeds however in words. The most difficult thing in life is to know yourself." — Thales

"Mental health is the ability to work and to love." —Heing Kohut

"As long as I'm trying to decide, I can't feel what I want to do." —Hugh Prather

"We need not pretend to understand the world only by intellect; we apprehend it just as much by feeling." —Carl Jung

"There is no desire when there is no feeling of want." —Plato

"You need to feel everything, otherwise the world loses its meaning." —Carlos Castaneda

Choose your favorite quotation, integrate it into your life **and then, watch what happens!**

> ***"I now repeat my favorite quotation three times a day."***

Write your favorite quotes.

_____

_____

_____

_____

_____

_____

_____

_____

_____

_____

_____

Do You Have Dreams?

What are some of your dreams for your life? Do you dream of better health, more money, a fulfilling career, a bigger house in an ideal location, a luxury or sports car, the latest fashion clothing, more friends, global travel, a dignified self-sufficient retirement, financial independence, more meaningful relationships, more time for yourself and family, peace of mind, a loving family or a deep spiritual belief system?

Just what do you dream about? Do you dream about your influence to create a world at peace? Is having more personal power important to you? Does acquiring in-depth knowledge, so you can make a great impact on the world, interest you? Do you dream of taking better charge of your life? Would you like helping people *BE* the best they can *BE*?

As you dream about your future lifestyle, are you willing to tell your friends about your dreams? If so, are you ready for the consequences?

When you tell your dreams to others, you may experience ridicule, criticism and possible abandonment. Have you ever been excited about your future, and then some people said, "Who do you think you are?" "You will never do that!" "So and so tried that and failed." "You start something and never finish." "I like you just the way you are, don't change." Basically, these comments are saying, "Stay in your box because I know you will never accomplish your dreams." When you hear these kinds of statements, how do you *feel?* Are you able to sustain your energy and interest? Do you allow people to destroy your dreams? I call that behavior "dream stealing."

Decide now to write down your dreams. Write them 20 times a day with *feeling.* Read them out loud at least three times a day. Tell no one your dreams, with the exception of your mentor. Focus on doing whatever it takes, without harming yourself or others, to move in the direction of your dreams. Read books, listen to audiocassettes, attend seminars and ask for help to acquire the skills you need. Find mentors who will encourage you and never shame you. Invest in building a powerful vocabulary so you can communicate with anyone.

Start a support group of four people who speak your language of success. Write your dreams in a journal.

Just as exercise and proper nutrition builds a strong, flexible body, I believe a daily investment in your competence moves you incrementally toward gradual realization of your dreams.

Take action now **and then, watch what happens!**

> *"I now choose to fulfill all of my dreams."*

How Can You Live A Healthier, Longer Life?

Have you decided how long you will live? Have you noticed that people are living longer? There are more then 35 million people over 60. Sociologists, faced with an aging population and increased life expectancy among people now over 65, are studying people who are 100 years old. *Research has found that moderation is the key to aging gracefully.*

In a survey of over 100 centenarians, psychologist Arthur Schuartz found:

1. They did not overeat or under eat.
2. They worked conscientiously. Yet, they were not workaholics.
3. Most of them slept about eight hours nightly.
4. They were moderate in exercise, sports and hobbies.

In another study, Northwestern Mutual Life Insurance Company asked its policyholders over 100 years old for their formula for a long life. They recommended:

1. Honesty.
2. Religious faith or an inner spiritual calm.
3. Vigorous physical activity.
4. Attention to diet.

Women continued to have a longer life expectancy of 79 years while men, on average, have the potential to live 72.3 years. Now that you are familiar with this data about life spans, how does it affect your point of view about your future?

Do you plan to do anything to make sure you will stay healthy for the rest of your life?

Proper nutrition, exercise and peace of mind seem to be the key ingredients to longevity. Naturally, you would expect me to say that intact Self-Esteem is absolutely essential to stay healthy and vibrant. Research continues to confirm the importance of intact Self-Esteem. Millions of people are investing in upgrading their attitudes about taking care of their health.

Decide now to give yourself permission to live a long and fulfilled life **and then, watch what happens!**

> *"I now focus on nutrition, exercise and Self-Esteem to increase my life span."*

"To Know
And
Not To Do
Is
Not To Know!"

Quote by William J. McGrane, CPAE

Chapter Seven

Your Mental Life

How Do You Handle Loss?

How do you *feel* about the national tragedies that involve death? This could include: airplane crashes, train wrecks, hurricanes, tornadoes, earthquakes or the death of a President, soldiers or astronauts,—where many citizens are in shock.

Shock is the first response when there is a critical incident which creates a significant emotional event. This critical incident could affect the entire world. The single most consoling thing, above all others, during this most shocking moment is for all people to share their grief. The second most consoling thing involves touching.

Dr. Elizabeth Kubler Ross has studied death and dying. In her book *Death—The Final Stage of Growth*, she discusses the stages of grieving, which are listed below.

1. Shock.
2. Denial.
3. Talking about the tragedy. *Feelings* need to be shared by all people involved. This is very important and includes the two essential communication skills of asking *feeling*-type questions plus external listening.
4. Depression.
5. Guilt.
6. Acceptance of the reality.

Each of these stages is important in the grieving process. You will also discover that it takes some people longer to grieve than others. It is also possible that some people may appear to be stuck in one of the stages. Listening and asking questions can serve best to help them move forward. Grieving is not meant to be rushed. Create a climate for you and others to grieve each stage at your and their own pace.

The more intact our Self-Esteem is, the easier it is to deal with the reality of death and dying or any other loss that we may experience. Intact Self-Esteem gives us permission to experience the full grieving process. Then we are ready to move ahead with our lives. It is healthy to talk about any loss.

When you experience a personal or national loss, begin the grieving process **and then, watch what happens.**

> *"I now grieve the losses in my life."*

How Do You Handle Anger?

Do you ever get angry? What do you want when you are angry? What does anger do for you? *Webster's Dictionary* defines anger as, "a *feeling* of displeasure resulting from injury, mistreatment or opposition, usually showing itself in a desire to fight back at the supposed cause of this *feeling*." We know that anger happens so quickly. So what do we know about anger?

Anger is an emotion. It is physically arousing and it affects your health. Anger is a *feeling*. It has an affect on the way you experience your world. Anger is a communicator. It sends information and a message to others. Anger is a cause. It produces specific affects and results.

Begin keeping a weekly record of each time you are angry. Write down the situations and circumstances that triggered your anger. Note the antecedents, that is, what happened right before you got angry? What was being said and done by others? What kind of internal dialogue was going on inside your head? Is the anger you *feel* a result of circumstances or situations outside of you, or is it the result of what is happening inside of you? Then write down the outcomes, the consequences of your anger. Evaluate your *feelings* and experience the energy drain from your body and your *feeling* of exhaustion.

People express their anger in a variety of ways: name-calling, criticism, pouting, revenge, violence, rage, absenteeism, loss of productivity, embezzlement, abandonment, addictions and bankruptcy. What is your number one way of letting your anger out?

Watch how often you get angry and the people or situations involved. You may want to record your observations in a journal. This procedure is called self-monitoring. The bottom line is that *anger immobilizes us and keeps us from moving forward.*

Is there a solution? The answer is "yes!" I believe there is a guaranteed way to overcome and eventually eliminate anger. The skill that needs to be developed is the ability to describe your *feelings!* This means you first need to learn and be able to identify your *feelings.* It is simple; however, it is not always easy. It takes "practice, rehearsal and drill." Self-Esteem is the self respect you *feel* for yourself. With intact Self-Esteem, you are able to communicate your *feelings* instantly to the other person involved. You can remain calm, relaxed and ask questions to communicate immediately that a solution is more important than verbal or physical violence. *Always pause for at least 30 seconds the moment you feel angry.* You will discover the power of the pause. It gives you the opportunity to relax and discover the wisest way to handle your anger to obtain elegant, exquisite and irresistible outcomes.

Decide that you want freedom from anger and invest in your Self-Esteem **and then, watch what happens!**

> *"I now pause when I feel anger and say,*
> *'I am calm and relaxed.'"*

Can You Release Anger?

Have you ever gotten angry? What makes you angry? Who makes you angry? How do you release your anger? Television and newspapers are filled with stories about the results of anger. When someone cuts in front of you with his or her car, do you get angry or do you say, "That's the way it is with that person right now"? The latter response helps you avoid labeling your *feelings* as anger. Is it easy to do? NOT ALWAYS! However, at that precise moment, you can evaluate your Self-Esteem by the way you act.

Did you ever have to wait for someone who is in the habit of being late? Were you angry or did you say, "That's the way it is with that person right now"? How could this be handled in a Self-Esteem manner? When you next meet with this person, create an advanced organizer, that is knowing what you need to do and say. You could say, "Bobbie, I have a challenge and I need your help. When I make an agreement, I keep my agreement. I enjoy our relationship and being with you; however, I *feel* uncomfortable when you are late. The next time we have an agreement to meet, I will wait for five (ten or fifteen) minutes after the agreed upon time. If by then you are not present, I will act as if our agreement has been canceled. Thank you for understanding, I appreciate your cooperation." This can be used with anyone in your family, business or socially. With this approach, you are honoring the other person(s) as well as yourself, and everyone's Self-Esteem is unharmed.

What is anger? It is a physical state of readiness. When we are angry, we are prepared to act. Physiologically what happens is this: more adrenaline is secreted, more sugar is released, our heart beats faster, our blood pressure rises and the pupils of our eyes open wide. We are highly alert. When we are angry, all of our energy is available. Anger is preparedness and power.

Of all of our emotions, anger can be the most dangerous to ourselves and to others. Anger can be your most unsettling enemy. Suppress it, and it could trigger a heart attack or stroke. Let it out in an unwise way, and it could ruin your marriage, your career, your business and your relationships. Use blame, guilt and/or punishment, and anger will never be resolved. Woody Hays, the Ohio State football coach, lost his job because of anger. What is the solution? Recognize your *feelings*, deal with them and be respectful of yourself and others.

Develop and refine your Self-Esteem skills **and then watch what happens.**

> *"I now release my anger the
> Self-Esteem way?"*

Are You Happy?

Is it easy for you to make up your mind? When you make a decision do you take action and fulfill your promise to yourself? Do other people know that about you? Would others say you are decisive and you act on your decisions?

Sparky Anderson, former Cincinnati Reds manager, predicted that Pete Rose would break Ty Cobb's record of 4,191 hits because Pete had the desire. He had made a decision to play baseball until he created the new record. Pete had skill, durability and mental toughness. He played until he surpassed the record. When Pete obtained his outcome of breaking the record, he was very happy and fulfilled.

How about you? Have you made up your mind to be happy? Evaluate these suggestions to determine if you are a happy person.

1. Decide what you want in order to be happy. Do you *feel* things, like a car or home, will make you happy? Do you *feel* people, like family or friends, will make you happy? Or will *you* make you happy?
2. Can you describe the challenges you may face during the process of becoming a happy person?
3. What are the payoffs for being happy? Will you be healthier, wealthier or wiser?
4. How many options can you develop daily to move closer to happiness?
5. Once you choose your alternative, will you decide to put it into practice?
6. Will you support yourself in carrying out your new decision? Will you have sustained energy?

It is important to remember that a wish and a decision are not the same thing. As you intensify your action program, will you focus on each step necessary to reach your outcome to be happy? Think of all of your habits. Are there any you want to change? Once you decide to start a new habit, then you can take action. With spaced repetition, you acquire new behavior. Your old habit will eventually fade away.

As you decide to be happy, there could be times when you prefer to be unhappy. That happens sometimes. Handle your unhappy *feelings* and then move forward again. *Happiness is a state of mind.* Nothing—no person, no thing, no place and no experience—can make you happy. Happiness is a do-it-yourself, inside job. Decide now to be happy **and then, watch what happens!**

> *"I now decide to be happy."*

Do You Live In The NOW?

Do you have a photo album? Have you saved pictures since you were born? What one fact stands out? After you read this message, go find your picture albums. As you review your life in pictures, think about this reality. Each picture of you and others was taken at one moment in time. I call that moment NOW!

In that moment, you may remember: what was going on in your life, where you were at that moment, your age, your weight and the style of clothes you wore. Since birth, up to this moment NOW, you have many pictures in your mind about your personal history. Do you remember the decisions you made in those NOW moments? Do you recall procrastinating or living in each present moment? Were you thinking about the past or the future rather than the present? What were the consequences of your indecision and not fully living in the present NOW? Do you *feel* as if you missed something?

Think about these deciding NOW moments: to study or not to study; to date or not to date; to speak or to be quiet; to marry or to remain single; to live at home with your parents or to begin your new life on your own; to laugh or to cry; to be happy or sad; to travel or stay home; to have high energy or low energy; to be self-centered or other-centered; to develop your talents or to settle for less; to have children or to make another choice; to read books or to avoid knowledge; to learn every day or to just dream about success; to find a mentor to help you would discover you; to dialogue with great minds by listening to cassette tapes or to be too busy; to volunteer your time for a worthy cause or to say, "Let someone else do it"; to develop your Self-Esteem daily; or to delay taking charge of your life.

Are moments important? Look at your pictures, the ones in your head as well as those in an album. Review your life and discover your most significant NOW moments. How would your life be different if these moments were missed? Evaluate where you are at this NOW moment. Are you more present to the NOW moment and with each person in the NOW moment? The only time to live is in the NOW moment. Even when you plan, schedule or write down outcomes you want in the future, the only time you can act on them is in the here and NOW moment.

Seize this moment and start acting in the NOW **and then, watch what happens!**

> *"I live my life in the NOW
> — in each moment."*

Have You Overcome Depression?

Do you know anyone who is depressed? Some people call it the blues. Dr. William Glasser, author of *Control Theory*, calls it "depressing." Dr. Glasser uses the verb *depressing* because it describes the total behavior. The noun *depression* only communicates the *feeling*. "The *feeling* component of a behavior is the largest and most obvious. The more we are able to recognize that it is just *one of the four components that make up our total behavior*, the more we will be in control of our lives." The other three components of any behavior are: doing, thinking and physiology. Dr. Glasser says, "It is impossible to choose a total behavior and not choose all its components."

In a *USA Today* newspaper article, Dr. William Zung said that he believes it is possible that you could be depressing and not know it. Dr. Zung says that some depressing symptoms may include forgetfulness and persistent loss of appetite. He has created a Self-Rating Depressing scale. Answer these statements by saying "none of the time," "some of the time," "a good part of the time" or "most of the time." Be aware that depressing can occur with those things we dislike as well as those we want and love. Here is a list for you to consider.

I *feel* downhearted, blue and sad. I *feel* best in the morning. I have crying spells or I *feel* like crying. I have trouble sleeping through the night. I eat as much as I used to. I enjoy talking to and being with members of the opposite sex. I notice that I am losing weight. My heart beats faster than usual. I get tired for no reason. My mind is as clear as it used to be. I find it easy to do the things I used to. I am restless and cannot keep still. I *feel* optimistic about the future. I am more irritable than usual. I find it easy to make decisions. I *feel* that I am useful and needed. My life is pretty full. I still enjoy the things I used to do.

As you evaluate the way you *feel*, be aware that your Self-Esteem determines how you take effective control of your life. Find people who value you. Listen to music that creates a comfortable mood. Exercise at least 30 minutes a day. Read self-development books. Listen to personal development tapes. Eat nutritional meals. Build your Self-Esteem daily. Dr. Glasser said, "To change a total behavior, the way you do it is to choose to change its *doing* and *thinking* components. Unless you choose to change what you do, think, or both—you will not change what you *feel*, because the total behavior of depressing makes good sense to you right now."

Decide now to own 100% of your personal power **and then, watch what happens!**

> *"I now cancel all depressing feelings and choose health."*

How Do You Handle Loneliness?

Have you ever been lonely? Have you ever been blue? That was the title of a popular song many years ago. Did you ever hear anyone say, "I have the blahs," or "Ugh—it's Monday morning"? Every day, millions of people experience *feelings* of loneliness. Then they *feel* stuck—immobilized—unable to move. When someone has *felt* lonely, then that same *feeling* becomes easier to repeat. Very often a choice is made to soothe pain with an artificial stimulant like drugs, alcohol or food. Loneliness is a painful experience. It is also an example of unintact Self-Esteem.

Research shows that when people are lonely, their instinct is to reach out to others, to touch someone. Newspaper columnist, Ann Landers did some research and found that women wanted more hugging. Men also want more hugging. If people have not been hugged, it is difficult for them to give or ask for a hug.

Just what is loneliness? How do we come to be lonely? What is happening in our lives that makes so many people lonely? There is a difference between loneliness and being alone. There are many ways to be alone and not lonely: one way is privacy, or seclusion for the purpose of quiet time. Then there is also constructive loneliness; that is when someone accepts responsibility that they cannot delegate to anyone else.

Charlie Brown, the Shultz cartoon character, said "The loneliest place on earth is the pitcher's mound during a baseball game." Ira Tanner says, "Loneliness is the fear of love." Abraham Lincoln *felt* lonely when he carried the weight of the world on his shoulders.

Another form of loneliness is withdrawal. People experience this when they have lost something precious—it has been withdrawn. This happens when people are afraid.

What is the solution to loneliness? All of the research says, "to know yourself" focus on only your affirming qualities. *Change your state of mind by focusing on others.* Reach out to other people—visit your favorite friend. Take a walk, call five people and tell them how much you appreciate them. Write your *feelings* in a journal. Sing your favorite songs. Dance.

Write to five people. Hang around people who are excited about life.

Get out of yourself, focus on others and give yourself away **and then, watch what happens!**

> **"I now reach out to others to find freedom from loneliness."**

Do You Practice Hospitality?

Do you know anyone who is lonely? Do you ever get lonely? Researchers have found millions of people who are lonely. Some people go to supermarkets, shopping centers and other places to find freedom from loneliness. In spite of the large crowds, some individuals become more lonely. What creates loneliness?

After all of my years of living, teaching, speaking and consulting, *I believe people are lonely because they lack skills.* In order to release loneliness they need to acquire the Art of Conversation, the Art of Listening, the Art of Asking Questions, the Art of People Reading and the Art of Reaching Out to Other People.

Loneliness is epidemic in our country. Loneliness lowers energy. Henry Now, in his book, *Reaching Out*, says, "Loneliness enters into everyone's life at some point. You might have *felt* it at some point as a little child when your classmates laughed at you, or as a teenager when you were the last one chosen for a baseball team. You might have *felt* it at work when no one spoke to you." Henry continues to say, "How is it that many parties and get-togethers leave us empty and sad? Too often we will do anything possible to avoid being alone." The solution, he says, is to *"reach out to your fellow human beings and learn the Art of Hospitality."*

Hospitality is a fundamental attitude of treating everyone you meet as a guest. It is a disposition where you treat people graciously, generously and kindly. Treat people like *royalty*.

This creates a free and friendly space for everyone. When this occurs, there are no strangers and you are excited to meet new friends.

Creating this space for others can be a challenging task, especially in the beginning. Be gentle, kind and patient with yourself. You are learning and practicing new behaviors. You are developing and refining new skills. With spaced repetition, these new skills and behaviors will gradually become second nature to you.

Begin by improving your Self-Esteem. When your Self-Esteem is intact, it is easier to treat everyone as a guest. Remember, at one time, even your best friend was unknown to you.

Reach out, ask questions and listen externally to discover more about the person in front of you **and then, watch what happens!**

> *"I now release loneliness by learning the Art of Hospitality."*

Have You Reached Out To Others?

Do you know any lonely people? Are you often lonely? What do you know about the runaways in today's world? Their average age is 15 and they are lonely people. They *feel* rejected and not included in the mainstream of life. They have a difficult time communicating with their parents. They drop out of school and often lose their thirst for learning for a lifetime. These runaways are filled with internal pain and have a difficult time describing their *feelings*. They have few skills they can sell for money, so they drift through life and allow themselves to be victimized. Their Self-Esteem is on the floor. Seldom do they meet someone who will become their mentor, someone who will affirm them to discover and develop their full potential.

When does loneliness begin? Dr. Tony Lake, author of the book *Loneliness*, believes it all starts with the circumstances in our life and then later with our personality. As you review the circumstances of your life, how close were you to your mother and father? How was their communication? What kind of interaction occurred in your home? Did you have the opportunity to describe your *feelings?* Were you included in conversations? Who listened and heard what you had to say? Were you valued as a child? Just where did you go to *feel* accepted? If there was no place to go as a child to be affirmed and valued, then where did you go when you grew up?

Review the past week, especially all the circumstances. Did you meet any lonely people? How did you respond to them? Were you able to have a conversation with them?

I once met a man who lost his mother, and 11 days later his father died. As we stood in the midst of a crowded airport, he thanked me for sharing with him the importance of communicating with parents. He said his father, before he died, touched him and his two sons for the first time in his life. This man cried publicly as he released his *feelings* of loneliness that had lasted for all of his 50 plus years.

Prepare now, by reaching out to everyone you meet, to help them to *feel* important because they met you. Begin with a smile or a nod of your head. Create 10 general questions you can ask anyone. Meet at least one new person a day. Do it now!

Make a significant impact on people **and then, watch what happens!**

> **"I now reach out to free someone from feeling lonely."**

Do You Relax and Enjoy Life?

Have you noticed how many people talk about the weather? People are concerned about snow, ice, temperature, rain and the sun. People's *feelings* can change because of their attitudes toward the daily weather. How do you *feel* about the daily weather changes? Do you *feel* any distress? Can you relax with the daily weather changes? Other potential areas for distress could be career or business changes, health, relationship tension and unrealized expectations. How do you handle distress?

We will all have distress as we journey through life. How can we relax and enjoy life? Here are some suggestions.

1. Clarify your values. Discover what is important to you. Ask yourself, "If I only had six months to live, what would I need to do, what would I want to do and how are my relationships?" Then for the rest of your life, focus on these things and forget about the pressures you and others put on you.

2. Learn to relax. How is this possible? All you need is a quiet room. Start by blotting out distractions for 10 to 15 minutes a day. Then build this up to a minimum of one hour of quiet time every day. Listen to mellow jazz or other relaxing music.

3. Be aware of your self-talk and improve it. We all talk to ourselves and much of it is self-critical. Discipline yourself to emphasize the things you like about yourself. A book that can help you know about self-talk is *What to Say When You Talk to Yourself* by Shad Helmstetter, Ph.D.

4. Exercise regularly. Check with your doctor first, and then find an exercise that you can do 3 times a week for 20 minutes each time.

5. Eat nutritious meals. Discover how to fuel your body with the nutrition it needs to operate for you at the highest level.

6. Create balance in all seven areas of your life: Social, Financial, Mental, Spiritual, Physical, Career and Family.

7. Release chemical dependency. One definition of *stress* is loss of control. The need to acquire control through artificial means accounts for the popularity of nicotine, alcohol, caffeine and drugs.

I believe that only with intact Self-Esteem can we find freedom from distress.

Decide now to make the next 12 months free from distress **and then, watch what happens!**

> *"I now relax and welcome each moment to build my Self-Esteem."*

How Do You Handle Worries?

When you were a child, what did you worry about? What did your parents worry about? Do you worry now? If so, what do you worry about? Are there any similarities between your parents' fears and your fears?

The *USA Today* newspaper did research on children's fears. Seven fears emerged. Here they are in order of importance.

1. School grades
2. The way they look
3. Their popularity
4. National hunger and poverty
5. National violence
6. Drugs and alcohol
7. Nuclear destruction

What are some of your worries? Are you worried about money, relationships, aging, your career or the future? Research shows that only eight percent of what people worry about ever happens.

What triggers worry? It is usually the absence of something. People can make themselves sick when they worry. We spend billions of dollars on sickness. That's a lot of worry about health. People who worry love to worry, and they love to get other people to love to worry. They infect other people. Misery loves company!

Worry prevents people from truly experiencing life. They are rarely present to the moment and each person in the moment. They worry about other people. They worry about the dark. They worry about being abandoned. They even worry about worrying. People who worry have unintact Self-Esteem. They deny themselves opportunities to release more of their potential. Their energy is drained by worrying.

People with intact Self-Esteem do not worry. So each day, as you meet challenges in your life, do what the song, *Sunny Side of the Street* suggests—develop your Self-Esteem and "leave your worries on the doorstep." Ask yourself, "What is the worst thing that can happen?" "What is the best thing that can happen?" Prepare for both, and then you will be able to handle anything that comes into your life. Give yourself permission to release your brakes and seize each moment. Live each moment to the fullest. *Take effective control of your life and all of your worries will disappear.* Remember, 92% of what you worry about never happens.

Learn to laugh at your worries **and then, watch what happens!**

> ### "I now leave all my worries on the doorstep."

Have You Let Go Of Your Fears?

Are you afraid of anything? What fears may be stopping you from being the person you want to be and living your life the way you want to live it? Fear can keep us from doing what we really, really, really, really, really, really, really want and need to do.

When fear holds us back, we experience *feelings* of confusion, self-doubt, frustration, anger and helplessness. Fears sabotage success. Are you afraid of flying, heights, water, bugs, elevators, public speaking, new situations, meeting new people, conversations or self-disclosure? The word *phobia* can be substituted for the word *fear*. A phobia is an irrational, persistent fear of a particular object or class of objects, which usually causes significant discomfort.

Fear is the painful emotion marked by alarm, dread, disquiet or a suggestion of these *feelings*. Fear is the anticipation of pain. There are three levels of fear.

1. Level One. These are fears of ordinary life events such as aging, retirement and being alone. It also includes the fear of taking action like going back to school, making decisions or changing a career level.

2. Level Two. These fears are situation-oriented. They involve the ego and things like rejection, success, loss of approval or helplessness. These fears involve the inner states of our mind.

3. Level Three. These fears get down to the nitty gritty of the issue. They are the ones that can keep you stuck. This is when you say, "I can't handle it." The truth is, if you knew you could handle anything that comes your way, what would you possibly have to fear? The answer is "nothing." All you have to do to diminish your fear is to develop more trust in your ability to handle whatever comes your way, and recognize that fear is merely the anticipation of pain.

As you look at the next 12 months, take a few minutes to evaluate what fears may be keeping you from being more productive and effective. Notice what *feelings* emerge. Observe, acknowledge and accept your *feelings* without judging them. *Feelings* are neither good, bad, right or wrong; they just "are"! When you judge or hold onto fear, you give yourself no choices. Fear controls your choices. With intact Self-Esteem, you can face your fear and take action, no matter how serious the fear may be. You will discover new ways of behaving. Eventually your easiest next step will be to face your biggest fear.

Begin to create intact Self-Esteem every day **and then, watch what happens!**

> *"I now develp my Self-Esteem to release my fears."*

Do You Name Call?

How do you *feel* about name calling? Did anyone ever call you a name? Have you called others names? How did you *feel*?

When I was in college, I labeled everyone. I called people "stupid," "idiot," "numskull" and many other names. Guess where I learned name calling? I heard other people do it. I never liked the *feeling* I had when I labeled people, and I did not like it when they labeled me.

Name calling feeds on itself. Anger, violence and wars are the result of escalated name calling. That is called value judging! Value judging is criticism, put downs—criticism of yourself, other people and situations. Once stated, these kinds of comments cannot be taken back. The words of regret have been said, yet the comments are not forgotten.

The United States has a value system. Every country has a value system. Each person has a value system. Everyone's value system is 100% affirming to them because it is their belief system. Wherever you go, you will meet people who have a different culture, do things differently and have a value system similar or different than yours.

The war of words is more powerful than any gun or other weapon. Every day someone tells me how they *felt* when they were a child, and their mother or father called them a name. Many people have carried this kind of childhood pain all of their lives. What is the solution? It is intact Self-Esteem. Yes, only intact Self-Esteem will cause someone to release value judging, name calling and criticism.

Name calling is the result of unintact Self-Esteem. Does that mean that anytime I call someone a name I have unintact Self-Esteem? Yes! How do you stop value judging and name calling? You do it by using affirming Self-Esteem language. Here are some suggestions.

Repeat these six affirmations for 30 days **and then, watch what happens!**

1. I now accept myself totally and unconditionally.
2. I now free myself from all self-destructive criticism.
3. I now give unconditional warm regard to all people at all times.
4. I now show that I am 100% alive by thinking, speaking and acting with great enthusiasm.
5. I now choose to be completely self-determined, and I allow others that same right.
6. I now release all comparisons with myself and others.

> *"I now release name calling*
> *and value judging."*

Do You Fight, Flee or Communicate?

Are you afraid of criticism? Do you recall the first time someone criticized you? Was it your mother, father, brothers, sisters, teachers, your friends or someone else? What did you do when you were criticized? What do you do now? Do you fight? Do you run away? Or do you stay and communicate?

With intact Self-Esteem, you respect yourself enough to stay and communicate. You recognize that often the criticism may have nothing to do with you or your behavior.

I once met a young man who *felt* like a nobody. He was criticized a lot. When he was criticized, he ran away. He became an outstanding student. He was a very intelligent person. When he went to work, he changed jobs often. One day he discovered the solution to his dilemma, which was to stay and communicate his *feelings*. However, because he had difficulty describing his *feelings*, he rejected the solution. He denied his *feelings* and continued to run away rather than choose peace of mind and tranquillity. This man's major learning experience is to communicate his *feelings*. Until he is able to do this, he will carry incompletions in his life; that is, he will continue to have similar agendas in his life. The consequence/outcome is pain, until he values himself enough to take charge of his life. Can you relate or identify with this young man?

Here are three questions to ask yourself or anyone to help deal with criticism.

1. How do you *feel* about what you did?
2. If you had it to do over again, what would you do differently?
3. How could I (or someone else) have helped you before you chose to take action?

We only criticize others to the degree we criticize ourselves. Freedom and peace of mind come when we learn to recognize and describe our feelings. Find people who know how to describe and communicate their feelings. Learn the skills necessary for superlative communication. Begin to explore your feelings. Write them down. Next, describe your feelings to someone who will listen to you without judging you or your feelings. As you become more aware of your feelings, you will also *feel* more fully alive, have more choices and your fears will dissipate.

Hang around people who treat you like royalty, so you can treat others like royalty **and then, watch what happens.**

> *"I now choose to stay and communicate*
> *regardless of the pain."*

Do You Release Criticism?

What disturbs you most about what is happening in the world? Is it drugs or other addictions? Is it violence? Is it hunger? Just what would you like to change? I once read in a newspaper article, "What makes your partner your worst critic?" The article mentioned that the most common social encounters are fraught with a thousand possible failures. Interpersonal relationships can be very fragile and delicate. For that reason, many people like to appear in public with partners—personal or business.

Every social encounter has the potential for blunders, sarcasm, criticism, put downs and/or value judging. Let's take criticism as a major issue. Were you criticized as a child? Were you called "dumb" or "stupid"? Were you compared to your bother or sister? Did teachers criticize you? Did your coach or friends criticize you? Now do you criticize your spouse, children, parents, fellow employees, business associates or boss? Are you hyper-critical of yourself? Do you call yourself "dumb" or "stupid"? Many of us have a tendency to criticize ourselves and those closest to us the most. Sarcasm is a common way to criticize.

I heard a member of a large family say, "The only way our family knew how to say 'I love you' was to be sarcastic." Sometimes I hear people say, "Oh, that was constructive criticism." *I personally believe all criticism is destructive.* With intact Self-Esteem, we learn to affirm and compliment people, especially people close to us.

All of us have blind spots. These are unconscious habits, defenses, ticks or other behavior. They are not known to us; however, they are known to others. Many people criticize us for these behaviors. The ideal outcome is "self-discovery." When people are patient with us and ask questions, we can discover our own blind spots. Only then are we ready to create new behavior.

You can make a difference in someone's life the Self-Esteem way. With intact Self-Esteem, you release criticism of yourself and others. It takes skill, time and practice, practice, practice. Life is a series of new beginnings. You may know someone who would like to learn how to stop criticizing. Encourage them to learn more about intact Self-Esteem.

Start now with new Self-Esteem skills **and then, watch what happens!**

> *"I now release all criticism and focus on building Self-Esteem"*

What Are Psychological Needs?

Will you have all of your needs fulfilled during any period of time? Have you saved your money to better guarantee that you will satisfy your financial needs? What if you do not satisfy these needs? What will you do? How will you *feel*? What percentage of those needs are material? What percentage are psychological?

This could be the time for you to review your six basic psychological needs. Each person, deep inside, *feels* the power of those six needs. If one of these needs is not satisfied, a deep-seated restlessness develops. It is like a vague unrequited longing and an undercurrent of disappointment that colors every minute of the day and night. Look at the number of teenagers and adults who *feel* helpless and hopeless. These are examples of people with unfulfilled needs. Let's review these six psychological needs.

Naturally, the first psychological need is for *Self-Esteem*. It is the self respect you *feel* for yourself. Everyone has intact Self-Esteem when they are born. Gradually Self-Esteem may be diminished by criticism and comparison. The loss of Self-Esteem has a lifetime effect on relationships and careers.

The second need is for *security*. The only security is internal security. Relationships, situations and careers may change. However, our inner security can accept any challenge.

Our third need is for *creative expression*. No one has fundamental happiness if they are not being creative in their leisure hours and their work.

The fourth basic psychological need is for *recognition*. Everyone needs to be appreciated. How often this week did someone say , "I appreciate you"? How often did you say it to someone? Every person needs to be regarded by someone as important and special.

The fifth need is for *new experiences*. Variety is the spice of life. How many new experiences will you create in the next few months?

The sixth need is for *love*. I believe love is T.U.A. (Total Unconditional Acceptance) of yourself and others. Take the time to review your life. Be gentle and kind with yourself as you discover where you are with each of these needs.

Satisfy these six basic psychological needs **and then, watch what happens!**

> *"I now satisfy my six basic psychological needs."*

How Is Your Creativity?

Are you creative? How convinced are you that your attitudes and Self-Esteem help you to be more creative? Would you like to improve your creativity? Here are some ways to do just that.

1. Invest in a creative journal. Write your ideas in the journal daily. Keep track of your ideas at all times. Carry a notebook wherever you go. Keep a notebook beside your bed. Ideas can come at strange times. Frequently, ideas come when we least expect them. The same idea may never come again. So, it is important to make a record of each idea right away. To facilitate this, you may want to carry a notepad and pen or micro-cassette recorder with you at all times. Listen to your hunches and intuitions, particularly during moments of relaxation—before going to sleep or upon awakening.

2. Ask new questions every day. A curious mind is a creatively active mind.

3. Learn about things outside of your specialty.

4. Be flexible. Notice your patterns of behavior. Find several solutions to each challenge. Discover new viewing points.

5. Be open and receptive to ideas. They can be fragile. Listen to them. Freely entertain apparently wild, farfetched or even silly ideas. This is part of the creative process.

6. Be alert in observation. Look for similarities, differences and unique and distinguishing features in objects, situations, processes and ideas. The more new associations and relationships you can form, the greater your chances are of coming up with really creative and original combinations and solutions.

7. Engage in hobbies. Especially develop hobbies that allow you to construct or produce something with your hands. Also, keep your brain trim by playing games, doing puzzles and tackling mental exercises.

8. Improve your sense of humor. Laugh easily. Humor relieves tension. You are more creative when you are relaxed.
9. Adopt a challenge-taking attitude. Nothing is more fatal to creativity than fear of failure.

So there you have it. Invest in your Self-Esteem to become more creative in your relationships and career **and then, watch what happens!**

> *"I now release my creativity to upgrade my relationships and career."*

How Do You Use Your Ideas?

Did you ever hear an idea and get excited about it? Did you ever tell other people about your idea, and then not take action to develop a plan to achieve success with it? Do you agree ideas abound everywhere? Do you *feel* that every person can think of a unique idea? Do you believe when a person is enthusiastic about his or her idea, that it is possible other people could want to kill the idea? Just what is it that causes such destructive thinking?

Let's look at an example. The McGrane Self-Esteem Institute exists for one reason—Global Self-Esteem. That is our mission—the outcome for our existence. We do this by giving keynote speeches, Self-Esteem programs, consulting and other special one-to five-day programs. People attend our programs from all 50 states. When they complete the sessions, they often go home all excited about the Self-Esteem principles. Most graduates recognize how the ideas can help them in their relationships and career. Many decide to integrate the information into their lives.

Very often the most significant people in their lives criticize or reject their new ideas and behavior. They usually are shocked by these rejections and sometimes question what they learned. They may hear such comments as, "Listen, I talked with you the day before you attended the Self-Esteem program. Don't tell me you have changed. You will never change. Those ideas will never work."

This is the moment of truth. It is time for belief, persistence and commitment. As you review history, you will find many individuals who have experienced rejection and criticism. Here are a few: Thomas Edison, Elizabeth Kubler-Ross, Henry Ford, Alexander Graham Bell, Margaret Mead, the Wright brothers and Virginia Satir. So what is the message about ideas? It is simple. The person with a burning desire and intact Self-Esteem does the following:

1. Gets rejected, yet does not *feel* rejected or take it personally.
2. Invests energy daily in moving forward.
3. Looks for resources to help create success.
4. Has a 15 year vision to integrate the idea.
5. Never gives up.
6. Is thirsty to be a role model for others.
7. Invests in a Lifelong Learning Program.
8. Is ready to commit to new ideas.

Take a stand, act now **and then, watch what happens!**

> *"I now choose an idea and develop*
> *it to completion."*

What Is Your Perception?

How do you see the world? How do you see your community? How do you see your family, your friends, your career and your life? Each person has his or her own perception of everything. If five people see the same event, there will be five different perceptions of it.

The first step in our adaptive behavior is how we obtain information about our environment. As we observe everything, we become aware that perception is an active and ongoing process.

Our daily decisions are greatly influenced by our perceptions. Perception is the awareness of objects, consciousness;

it is direct acquaintance with anything through the senses. As we experience consequences, based on our decisions, we learn about the intensity of the signals we receive to make our daily choices. Sometimes, the way we perceive things can cause us to make choices that do not serve us or others. We can only perceive one thing at a time. Whatever we perceive with the greatest intensity generally gets our attention. However, we can have many distractions and invitations to make different choices. The more information we have about something, the easier it is to make a decision about whether to move in a particular direction.

Our needs, wants, values, past experiences and current state of mind affect the clarity of our decision making. Our five senses influence the intensity of our perceptions. At any moment we experience a vast array of sensory stimuli. We cannot attend to all the distractions at once. We can only attend to a limited number of stimuli at one time. The mind can only hold seven, plus or minus two, pieces of information at one time. We always need to make specific selections.

What does the topic of perception have to do with Self-Esteem? It's simple. Your investment in building your Self-Esteem is influenced by the intensity—the power of your perception. Namely, your efforts to learn and apply these principles will depend largely on your perception of how unintact or intact Self-Esteem meets your needs, wants and values. Your behavior, and the outcomes you receive, will tell you the clarity of your perception, whether your Self-Esteem is intact or unintact.

Observe and evaluate your perceptions from a Self-Esteem viewing point **and then, watch what happens!**

> *"I now intensify my perception to
> focus on my Self-Esteem."*

How Often Do You Read?

Do you watch the changes from winter to spring? Does the spring season remind you of baseball and of getting outside to enjoy nature? Does it remind you of new beginnings? Does it remind you of spring cleaning? How about letting it remind you of new, Lifelong Learning skills for your future success and happiness?

Once I spoke about communication and Self-Esteem to an automotive die casting company in Detroit, Michigan. Many employees attended this all day seminar to build better communication skills. At the end of the day, two young men approached me. One said, "I divorced my wife because she was learning more about herself by reading, playing cassette tapes and attending seminars. What a mistake I made. I now know that she was personally growing. If only I had been more curious." The second young man said, "I cannot read. All my life I have been filled with tension because I never learned to read. As of today," he said, "I will learn to read."

These are just two examples of the kinds of behavior I hear from people I meet every day. Research shows that approximately 80 million people in the United States are illiterate or have poor reading skills. They did not learn to read in school, so now they settle for less in their relationships and career. Can you appreciate how difficult it would be to just get around a city if you could not read street signs? How can a person fill out a job application without reading? What impact does illiteracy have on parents when their children begin to read and ask for help?

Few people realize the damaging effects illiteracy has on their Self-Esteem. People who cannot read often *feel* "less than." They are often treated with less dignity and respect. People who are illiterate may want to learn how to read; however, they are often afraid to admit their ignorance. Reading allows people to expand their awareness and *learn the knowledge necessary* to obtain any skill desired.

Do you like to read? Do you read a book a week or a book a month? Is reading a part of your daily menu? Are you interested in developing your personal and professional skills? Is it possible that reading can serve you and others in acquiring these skills? Do you give books as gifts? Do you recommend books to others? Have you acquired your own library? Is there a library card in your wallet? Have you introduced children to the library? Do you read to children? Do you encourage children to read?

Now is the time to give yourself a spring reading skills checkup **and then, watch what happens!**

> *"I now read 30 minutes every day."*

Can You See With New Eyes?

Do you appreciate your gift of sight? Do your realize that your eyes can communicate instant rejection or acceptance? When you complete reading this message, find a mirror and look into your eyes. See if your eyes are hard or soft. See if your eyes are stressed or calm. See if your eyes are cold or warm. Can you see if you repel or attract people with your eyes?

As you look into your eyes, visualize your mind as a slide projector with an infinite number of slides stored in its library. It is an instant retrieval system with an endless cross-referenced subject catalog. Turn on your slide projector and see your entire life and all the pictures you have collected in your picture library.

See those critical moments which created significant emotional events. See what you did since those moments. Are you sad? Are you happy? Do you wake up each day and see ugliness or do you see beauty? Do you see sickness or do you see health? Do you see enemies or do you see friends? Do you see scarcity or do you see abundance?

Every moment you have a choice—to have intact Self-Esteem or not. One of the most important ideas in the 20th Century is the power of visualization—the power to see the kind of lifestyle you want. Visualization puts power into your eyes which can profoundly affect your life.

When you see the world around you—you call it reality. When you see the world in your mind's eye, what is it? It is visualization. Valerie Wells notes in her book, *The Joy of Visualization*, that "visualization is simply the process of creating pictures in your mind; it gives form to your thoughts so you can more easily direct them toward a specific outcome. You may have more of a sense, or a *feeling*, of it than an actual picture." Be assured all of these are visualizations. It is one of our most basic processes. Human beings program self and others through pictures—the mind's eye. For example, when you see a TV commercial, the advertiser is attempting to program your unconscious mind into buying the product or service. Visualization is the ultimate conscious tool.

Start to appreciate your eyes and your power to visualize **and then, watch what happens!**

> **"*I now appreciate my eyes which see the beauty in the world.*"**

How Open Is Your Heart?

Do you remember the song, *You Gotta Have Heart*—"all you really need is heart"? I named the McGrane Self-Esteem Institute on Valentine's Day 1977. After 40 years of qualitative research on Self-Esteem, I had my biggest breakthrough, my greatest Aha, my most profound insight about how to build my own Self-Esteem. I now know that building Self-Esteem takes a lifetime. I can never take a vacation from my Self-Esteem because I am always aware of the respect I *feel* for myself.

I know I need to take care of my heart because the heart is the life-giving pump. The rhythm of the heart allows the brain to think, the lungs to breathe and the muscles to move. The heart is the center of life. The Book of Proverbs says, "a merry heart maketh a cheerful countenance; however, by sorrow of the heart the spirit is broken." The more intact your Self-Esteem, the easier it is to have T.U.A. (Total Unconditional

Acceptance) for all people, free of value judging and comparisons. Here is a story by Fairfax Douney called "The Human Heart."

The Light of the World is a beautiful painting which was created by Holman Hunt. It is a painting of Christ in a garden at midnight. In His left hand He is holding a lantern; with His right hand He is knocking on a heavily paneled door. On the day the painting was unveiled, a group of art critics were present. As the curtain was drawn aside, one of them approached the artist and said, "Mr. Hunt, how come you have not finished your work?" "It is finished," the artist answered. "However, there is no handle on that door," the critic pointed out. "That," said the artist, "is the door of the human heart and it can be opened only from the inside."

This week, how will you open your heart from the inside? Send a thank-you note to your father, mother, teacher or friend. Buy a rose and send it to someone who believes in you, and write on the card, "A rose says it all." Give a hug to five people and give them your undivided attention for two minutes each. Speak to five new people during the next week. Smile when you speak to people. Help five people *feel* better about themselves because they met you.

Open your heart from the inside **and then, watch what happens!**

> *"I now open my heart from the inside."*

Chapter Eight

Career

Do You Strive For Excellence?

Are you an excellent achiever? Did you ever watch the Olympic achievers? Only one person wins the Gold Medal; only one person wins the Silver Medal; and only one person wins the Bronze Medal for each event.

How do you *feel* about your own level of achievement at this time of your life? Just what is *achievement?*

To achieve means to overcome obstacles and accomplish difficult things. The achieving person is one who exhibits a high degree of striving, excellence and success.

People who are excellent achievers tend to: seek out and enjoy challenges, work hard in a smart way, make acceptable grades and advance their education or knowledge in their areas of interest.

The more intact your Self-Esteem, the more you achieve because you no longer compete with other people. Since you only compete with yourself, you are free of comparison, and you have the energy to be more curious about everything in your life. As a result, you are more teachable; you study more; you learn more skills; you maximize your potential; and you are outcome oriented.

In contrast with people who are driven to achieve, psychologists have found that many other people are motivated by fear of failure. They compare themselves to others. They settle for less and *feel* like victims. Very often these people live a life of dependence, to one degree or another, rather than take charge of their lives.

As you watch the Olympic achievers, does their commitment to and show of excellence compel you to upgrade your competence?

How much more competent will you be 5, 10, 15 years from now? What excellence will you acquire in the seven areas of life: social, mental, physical, financial, spiritual, career and family?

John Gardner, in his book *Excellence*, said, "Our society cannot achieve greatness unless individuals, at various levels of ability, accept the need for high standards of performance and strive to achieve those standards within the limits possible for them."

Decide now to upgrade your Self-Esteem, and you will become an excellent achiever **and then, watch what happens!**

> *"I now strive to achieve excellence daily."*

What Is The "And Then Some Principle"?

Have you ever heard of the "And Then Some Principle"? Are there people who work with or for you whose attitude is: "Don't do too much. Just do what you get paid for and no more"?

When I was in college, I worked part-time on the railroad, in a warehouse, in a brewery and also in a produce company. Since all the employees knew I was a short term worker, I was frequently told not to work too hard. They knew they would still be there after I left and did not want a new standard set.

Would you agree many workers need and want more money to satisfy a comfortable lifestyle? Do you know people who want a promotion? What can be done to help people acquire the money and promotions they say they want?

The "And Then Some Principle" says that you do what you are paid to do "And Then Some."

The next time you call your favorite store, notice the tone of voice of the person who answers the phone. If you have a challenging situation that needs to be resolved, observe how long it takes you to obtain a solution.

Hear the words the person uses to communicate with you. Listen for courtesy, concern and enthusiasm—that's the "And Then Some Principle." Then focus on *your* telephone skills. If someone were evaluating your telephone competence, would they recommend that you be given a raise or a promotion?

Your voice has the power to turn people on or off. Would your voice cause others to want what you have to offer? There are three basic voice tones you can choose when conversing. You can use a soft voice, your normal voice or a command voice. Each is acceptable. The skill is knowing what voice is appropriate for the situation. For example, if a person was about to run in front of a car, you would use your command voice to save his/her life.

When you listen to a speaker, watch television or go to a movie, notice the power the voice has in creating an impact on you. Listen to hear the "And Then Some Principle."

Recall the voices from your past. Whose voices do you remember? How did you *feel* when you listened to them: comfortable or uncomfortable?

Decide now to develop your voice to create a climate of acceptance. Refuse to yell or scream at anyone. Soften your voice whenever another person is upset or angry.

For the next week invest in improving your voice **and then, watch what happens!**

> *"I now believe in the "And Then Some Principle" by doing more!"*

How Do You Create Your Career?

Do you know what you need, want and value? Will you know it when you see, hear and *feel* it? All of us have a personal history. This is made up of our heredity, our intuition and our total life experiences (which includes our environment). Based on our personal history, we develop a degree of skill of getting along with people at home, at work, in business and socially.

As we interact with people, we create either mutually beneficial empathic relationships or some degree of conflict. The newspapers and television are filled with stories of violence, unaffirming behavior and different kinds of addictions. All of us have experienced *feelings* of unintact and intact Self-Esteem.

What would need to exist to create an environment where people could thrive and work together in harmony? For over forty years I have qualitatively researched the subject of Self-Esteem. I have found that a critical area for people is their career. Many high school and college graduates will have difficulty finding a job. Some workers are released from their jobs and face the challenge of interviewing with companies, expecting to find employment quickly. Others are choosing to become entrepreneurs by starting their own businesses.

The reality is companies are more selective now than ever because of their need for competence, specific skills and a constant eye on the bottom line. Beside technical skills, workers and entrepreneurs need people skills and interviewing skills to succeed.

If you ever find yourself in any of these situations remember, *Never settle for less.* Your security is within you. You have the ability to do whatever it takes to create the outcomes you want! Now is the time to create your career. Webster defines career as: "Course of a person's life, especially in some particular pursuit. The notable or conspicuous progress or success in one's chosen calling." Therefore, everyone has a career. The question is: "Have you made a conscious decision to create your career the way you want it?" Careers include: parent, lawyer, guard, street person, receptionist, entrepreneur, paramedic, ditchdigger, teacher, sales person and thousands of others. Make a decision, make it your own and make it now to create a career that blends with your purpose in life. Then you can pursue the job, work, or position, including being an entrepreneur, that will give you the outcomes you want in your career and life.

As you interview, ask questions to discover how your philosophy blends with the person or organization. Notice the energy level. Is this person or organization creating a climate of acceptance? Are you and others being treated with dignity and respect? Are you given undivided attention during this conversation? Are all people present asking questions to discover how everyone can work together in harmony? Does everyone have the people skills and intact Self-Esteem to be able to accept a match or mismatch?

Take charge of your life. Create your lifestyle and career the way you want it **and then, watch what happens!**

> *"I now upgrade my interviewing and people skills to make my best career choice."*

Do You Negotiate Or Strike?

Have you ever heard people talk about going on strike? Have you seen headlines about strikes? Do you know someone who will be affected by a strike? Do you believe that many people fear strikes: employees, management, families, other businesses and communities? Did you ever wonder what creates a strike?

I believe that strikes are caused by employees' and management's lack of skills and/or their unintact Self-Esteem to negotiate and compromise. It seems that we, as a society, have learned very little from history. After every war, there is negotiating and compromising.

A strike is an indication that both management and employees need to communicate their needs, wants and concerns on an ongoing basis. They need to be continually establishing a mutually beneficial relationship.

All events in our lives go through a process called gradualism. A child grows into an adult by the body, mind and spirit changing through the years. It is a process and it varies for each individual.

Business and organizations develop in similar fashion. There is birth, infancy, childhood, the teen years, young adulthood, adulthood, maturity and the vintage years. It does not happen overnight. It is a process. Along the way there is always a moment when employees and management become aware of their needs, wants and values. If there is a conflict concerning how these are to be met and fulfilled, then resolution needs to take place. *When people are deprived of a need at the point of its highest intensity, they will have it met at some other time, in some other way.* This could include: sabotage, slowdowns, sickness, quitting or strikes.

With intact Self-Esteem, there is never a desire to strike because people will communicate at a level where both parties talk about their needs, wants and values. They will initiate negotiating and compromising appropriately to establish mutually beneficial results. Employees and management will listen to everyone's point of view and be able to create a viewing point that is mutually beneficial.

What is the real fear that causes a strike? I believe it is the fear of losing control. Employees want to maintain or achieve a dignified lifestyle. Management wants to stay in business and make a profit. Either or both may perceive that their wants will be infringed upon or ignored.

Strikes would not occur if both groups had intact Self-Esteem and were willing to negotiate and compromise. In the end, both parties will do it anyway. Does it make sense to negotiate and compromise up front? I believe so. Before there is even any sign of discomfort or miscommunication, continuing dialogue is necessary.

Do you ever go on "strike" with your friends, your family, your company, your own business or your associates? All strikes could end when: people are *sensitive* to the needs, wants and values of each other; they invest *time* in cultivating harmonious *relationships;* they *initiate* describing their uncomfortable *feelings* with each other; they *upgrade* their *people knowledge and skills;* and they keep their *Self-Esteem* intact.

So the next time you hear about a strike, remember the words: sensitivity, time, relationships, initiate, knowledge, Self-Esteem; and activate them **and then, watch what happens!**

> *"I decide to avoid all strikes by negotiating and compromising now."*

Have You Investigated Great Minds?

Are you an idea person? What is your best idea so far this year? Once you get an idea, how long does it take you to act on the idea?

There has never been anything with more powerful potential than an idea in the mind of a single person. Einstein was a man who ate like other men and washed his face like other men. Yet, with the thinking of his mind, we have been able to top the ultimate source of energy in nature. Ideas are a dime a dozen. It's the idea that is acted upon which can make a difference. I was reading a book recently about the thirty minds that shaped our civilization. How many of these Great Thinkers do you recognize?

Jesus	Aquinas	Newton	Clerk Maxwell	
Moses	Columbus	Rousseau	William James	
Confucius	Machiavelli	Kant	Nietysche	
Plato	Copernicus	Malthus	Pavlov	
Aristotle	Luther	Clausewity	Freud	
Euclid	Bacon	Darwin	Einstein	Wiener
Augustine	Descartes	Marx	Keynes	Sartre

There are also many women who have impacted the world. See how many of these Great Thinkers you recognize:

Sappho	Eleanor Roosevelt
Hildegard of Bingen	Karen Horney
Sacajawea	Ruth Benedict
Margaret Fuller	Anna Freud
Harriet Beecher Stowe	Margaret Mead
Susan B. Anthony	Hannah Arendt
Elizabeth Blackwell	Rachel Carson
Emma Curtis Hopkins	Mary Leakey
Marie Curie	Virginia Satir
Maria Montessori	Shirley Chisholm
Mary McLeod Bethune	Elisabeth Kubler-Ross
Helen Keller	Barbara Jordan

There you have it—54 great thinkers. How many of these individuals and their contribution(s) to the world do you recognize? Whose ideas make the most sense to you? How have those ideas impacted your life? Who are some of the other great thinkers you would like to investigate? Do you want to be a great thinker? What do you want to leave behind to grow?

Every day as you decide how to be productive, evaluate all of your ideas and then take action. What career ideas will you use today to maximize your potential? What book will you read today to improve your productivity? What audio or video cassette will you play today to upgrade your competence? What education course or seminar will you experience to invest more deeply in career knowledge?

Decide now to invest in great ideas **and then, watch what happens!**

> *"I now invest in great ideas of great thinkers, including mine."*

How Does Your Self-Esteem Influence Your Career Success?

What did you want to be when you grew up? Did you want to be a doctor, lawyer, businessperson, mother or father? Did you want to be a lifetime student? Did you want to be a teacher? Did you want to be a person with intact Self-Esteem?

People with intact Self-Esteem accept responsibility for everything they think, say, do and *feel*. People who have intact Self-Esteem like themselves regardless of the rejection, indifference or criticism they receive from others. People with intact Self-Esteem ask questions to show their interest in others. People with intact Self-Esteem listen to others and give them their undivided attention. People with intact Self-Esteem have great energy. People with intact Self-Esteem are team players. They help others succeed. People with intact Self-Esteem accept others totally and unconditionally. People with intact Self-Esteem are committed to a cause bigger than life. People with intact Self-Esteem share their wisdom and skills with others. People with intact Self-Esteem are at peace with themselves. People with intact Self-Esteem can see the humorous side of life. People with intact Self-Esteem help others *feel* important.

Do you meet many people who have intact Self-Esteem? One way you can tell about a person's Self-Esteem is the way they focus on people. They create an atmosphere that is safe, secure and comfortable.

What about the management where you work? Do they have intact Self-Esteem? You can tell by how easy it is to talk with them. Do they create an atmosphere of acceptance? Can you speak freely about your pay, working conditions, learning opportunities, skills, benefits, etc.? Are you encouraged to be congruent (your words, *feelings* and behavior are in agreement) without fearing the loss of your job or career advancement? Just because a person is financially successful or holds a respected position, does not necessarily mean that he or she has intact Self-Esteem. Behavior will always let you know if a person's Self-Esteem is intact.

Is your present pathway moving you toward your ultimate ideal career? Would you say your work/career makes a difference? Are you fulfilled with what you are doing? How do you *feel* about having your child follow in your footsteps? Have you ever taken the time to write your own work/career plan? Are you on purpose with your work/career or are you following someone else's vision?

Take some time to review and write down your career history. Begin with any job you had where you earned money. This includes paper routes, baby-sitting, cutting grass, cleaning house, taking out the trash, etc. Write what you liked best and least about each job. What were your greatest qualities as a worker? How did you acquire these skills? Were there any skills you wanted to refine or develop? Who were your favorite bosses? What was it about their behavior that caused you to like working with them?

Based on where you are today, what are your five top skills? What areas do you want to refine? If you were someone else, would you want to be your employee or employer? Are there any characteristics you would like to acquire to be an excellent employee, employer or entrepreneur?

Prepare a plan to obtain better career results **and then, watch what happens!**

> *"I now evaluate my career history and plan new strategies for career success."*

Do You Clarify Your Values?

How do you *feel* about how business operates today? Do you like the way employees are being treated? What about productivity? How about quality? Do you like your company's management practices? Do you like your organization's style?

Today's businesses and organizations need managers, leaders and workers with new skills and competencies to improve their performance in a world where major changes are occurring at an increasing rate.

It is time to create organizations with intact Self-Esteem practices which produce powerful short and long term results. This means bringing out the best in people.

Here are some of the Self-Esteem characteristics needed in organizations.

1. The organization's values are known and practiced.
2. The focus is on results with the dignity and respect of people being intact.
3. Accountability is managed in a respectable, congruent manner by everyone.
4. People are recognized, appreciated and affirmed for who they are as people.
5. There is a supportive environment and mentoring system.
6. Each member of the organization has intact Self-Esteem.

The key component in creating an intact Self-Esteem organization is its values. They are views that are important to individuals or companies, held consciously or unconsciously, that are desirable and ethical. Value statements provide direction for the organization and individuals. They are best communicated both verbally and in writing. Values provide standards by which people are influenced in their choices of actions. Values are the basis for deciding what one is for or against or where one is going and how come. Values give direction to our lives and help us establish our character. Our values influence our basic ways of behaving in relationship with others and our environment. Acknowledgment and support of an organization's values can create a unifying force both inside and outside the organization.

From only a few dozen basic values, people's attitudes and beliefs flow and are experienced as actions relative to some subject, issue or situation. Values are subjective and become observable through language, the words being used. Values are only reflected in behavior when individuals or organizations meet their needs. Congruence then occurs because the words and behavior go together; they are the same. Only then do we believe that individuals and organizations are *living their values*.

Take a few moments now to discover your values. Write down that which is desirable and ethical for you. When you complete the list, note, by numbering one through five, which are your top five values. Review these top five values to determine whether what you say and do are the same. If you are not acting on your values, it is because you have not yet learned how to meet your needs.

Take the steps necessary to live your values **and then, watch what happens!**

> *"I now clarify my values to see if they are in harmony with the values of my organization."*

Would You Ask Yourself 22 Questions For A Quantum Leap?

How do you *feel* about your job or career? How do you *feel* about this year so far? Are you making the kind of progress you wanted? When was the last time you gave yourself a checkup? Here are some questions for you to consider in giving yourself a life balance checkup.

1. What was the most recent advancement, promotion or raise you received at work?

2. Have you written down the outcomes you want for your life?
3. What was the latest discovery you made about the nature, potential or talent of someone in your immediate family?
4. What two achievements would you like to accomplish this year?
5. Do you recall the last important discovery you made about yourself? What was it and what did you do with it?
6. What specific five-year outcome do you want in each area of life: financial, social, mental, spiritual, physical, career and family?
7. What will you do in the next 12 months to make a difference in your job or career?
8. What is your latest personal creative effort?
9. When did you last write a poem, paint a picture or create something?
10. What are your best work skills and abilities?
11. What are the attributes that contribute to your success?
12. How many books did you read in the last 12 months relating to your career or personal development?
13. Do you listen to music for motivation and to help you relax?
14. How many audio cassettes did you listen to in the last year relating to your career or personal development?
15. What are the three biggest challenges you currently face in your career?
16. Who do you admire most for their accomplishments?
17. Who do you admire most for their sensitivity?
18. What was the last project you carefully planned and executed?
19. What is the last completely spontaneous thing you can remember doing?
20. What is the most important thing you accomplished last week?
21. What major learning experience will you choose for next year to increase your competence, effectiveness and Self-Esteem?

22. What is the most playful or silly thing you did last week? Take action now **and then, watch what happens!**

> *"I now ask myself questions to prepare for a quantum leap to create balance in my life."*

Are You Proficient At The Art Of Asking Questions?

Have you ever wondered how come I ask so many questions? When you were a young child did anyone say: "Stop asking so many questions. It's none of your business. Don't be so nosy! People don't like you when you ask questions"? For that reason, are you afraid to ask questions now? Are you uncomfortable when someone asks *you* questions?

Remember when you applied for a job—all the questions you were asked. As you review your past 5, 10, 15 years, how do you *feel* about your work and career? Are you satisfied? Are you fulfilled? Are you ready for the "what ifs"?

1. What if I don't like my job, career or business?
2. What if I lose my job, career or business?
3. What if I don't like my boss?
4. What if the organization downsizes?
5. What if I don't like my organization?
6. What if I became physically incapacitated?
7. What if I don't enjoy going to work anymore?
8. What if my company merges or is sold?
9. What if I don't get along with my co-workers or staff?

What other questions have you asked yourself to prepare for the "what ifs"? Have you decided how much money you want to earn this year? Do you have the plans and action table for that once in a lifetime dream vacation? Have you chosen the date for your next promotion or career outcome? Do you invest in a Lifelong Learning Program to upgrade your skills? Are your children's education funds in place? How is your retirement portfolio?

Would the answers to these questions serve you in creating your life the way you want it? Are you concerned about some areas of your life? Would you like to learn the most important communication skill that would help you with your career and relationships? Are you interested in improving your conversation skills? Is it important for you to be comfortable when you meet new people? Are you interested in acquiring the skills that are necessary to be in charge of your life?

If you answered "yes" to any of these questions, then I invite you to develop and refine your Art of Asking Questions skills **and then, watch what happens!**

> *"I now decide to upgrade my skills*
> *of Asking Questions."*

What About Meetings?

Do you attend and/or conduct meetings? Are the meetings well planned? How many quality meetings have you attended or conducted? The next time you meet, ask these questions. Did you define beforehand what you expected the meeting to achieve? What outcomes did you want?

The purpose of the meeting could be to communicate facts. If so, a straightforward talk or lecture could be the best method because it saves time. It is important to allow time for questions and discussion. The purpose of the meeting could also be to influence attitudes. For example, you may choose to create a climate of acceptance by working with the group, which can help people be self-motivated. You may also attend or conduct a meeting to train people to develop skills. You may want to resolve a challenge by encouraging the group members to develop their own answers, thereby improving cooperation and trust.

As you observe the group, what is your evaluation of their participation? Do all members show intact Self-Esteem by their ability and willingness to describe their opinions and *feel-*

ings? With intact Self-Esteem, people are free of the status and power games which prevent integrative dialogue. All participants deserve whatever encouragement is needed to create a climate of acceptance so they share their ideas.

Next, what is the pre-planned agenda ? What activity is to be covered? All business needs to be covered. The meeting leader's responsibility is to complete the agenda and to summarize at the end of the session. It is possible that at the completion of the meeting there will be new unfinished business, like additional research that is needed. However, each agenda item needs to be given full attention.

The final question in an excellent quality meeting is, "What did you learn from the meeting and what action will you take?" The real payoff will depend on the follow-up after the meeting. You will have more receptive participants attend meetings now and in the future when:

1. You start on time and end on time.
2. An agenda is given to each person.
3. Full participation is realized.
4. Intact Self-Esteem behavior is modeled.
5. All participants are recognized for their contributions.
6. Participants see results.

Plan your excellent quality meetings well **and then, watch what happens!**

> *"I now plan all meetings to gain*
> *cooperation and trust."*

Are You Constantly Upgrading Your Skills?

Did you ever wonder what skills are needed to be President of the United States? Do you believe the Presidency is the most challenging job in America? How can one person carry out all the responsibilities? Do you agree Americans want their President to succeed?

Take a few minutes to evaluate and list your skills. Then consider what skills organizations want from their employees. Beyond basic reading, writing and computation skills, organizations expect competence in creative thinking, personal management, leadership and interpersonal relations. The abilities to organize and verbalize thoughts, conceptualize, resolve conflicts and work in teams are also critical.

The workplace often requires employees to have more than the standard academic requirements. Organizations also want people to have other key basic skills. These skills provide a foundation for building broader, more sophisticated skills. These key basic skills include:

1. Learning to Learn—the ability to acquire the knowledge and skills needed to learn effectively, regardless of whether the learning situation is ideal or not.
2. Listening—the ability to carefully consider the concerns and issues raised by customers, clients, suppliers, co-workers, employees and associates (current and potential).
3. Oral Communications—the ability to describe your thoughts and *feelings*.
4. Problem Solving—the ability to "think-on-your-feet."
5. Creative Thinking—the ability to come up with innovative ideas and solutions.
6. Self-Esteem—the self respect you *feel* for yourself.
7. Knowing the Outcomes You Want—that which comes out of or results from something else. In this case, it is the ability to be self-motivated in adjusting behavior to acquire results with integrity for self and others.
8. Personal and Career Development Skills—an awareness and possession of the skills needed to perform well.
9. Interpersonal Skills—the ability to get along with customers, suppliers, co-workers and associates.
10. Teamwork—the ability to work with others to achieve agreed-upon outcomes.
11. Negotiation—the ability to build consensus through giving and receiving.
12. Organizational Effectiveness—the understanding of where the organization is headed and how you can

make a contribution, individually or in cooperation with others.

13. Leadership—the ability to accept responsibility for creating a climate of unconditional acceptance where customers, clients, suppliers, coworkers and associates can motivate themselves to take action.

Evaluate and upgrade your basic skills to invest in your career success **and then, watch what happens!**

> **"I now upgrade my skills daily."**

Are You An Effective Leader?

Are you a leader? What is your definition of a leader? Who is your leader role model? My definition of a leader is simple— **a leader is someone who has followers.** Let's look at some of the traits of an effective leader.

Leaders possess the following traits: alert to the social environment, ambitious and achievement oriented, cooperative, dependable, decisive, energetic, self-motivated, persistent, tolerant of stress, willing to accept responsibility, self-disciplined and visionary. They know how to delegate, adjust to situations and influence others with honesty and integrity.

Effective leaders have very specific skills such as: they are intelligent and conceptually skilled, they are creative, they are diplomatic and tactful, they are articulate and speak fluently, they are knowledgeable about group tasks, they are socially skilled, they are organized and they have administrative ability.

AT&T conducted a study on the most effective leadership traits. The study revealed all leaders had the following 16 characteristics:

1. Oral communication skills
2. Need for advancement
3. Tolerance of uncertainty
4. Decision making skills
5. Wide range of interests
6. Ability to delay gratification
7. Internal work standards
8. Integrity with self
9. Human relation skills
10. Resistance to stress
11. Organizing skills
12. Creativity
13. Behavioral flexibility
14. Need for security
15. Planning skills
16. High energy

How many leadership traits and skills do you have? Is it possible that these skills and traits can serve you in all areas of your life? Are you interested in acquiring, refining or upgrading your leadership traits and skills? I believe the number one skill needed to be an effective leader is intact Self-Esteem. Developing your Self-Esteem is the best way to adjust to situations where there is resistance to you, your style or your ideas.

With intact Self-Esteem you can become a leader who will create an environment where people can thrive **and then, watch what happens!**

> *"I now learn to be an effective leader with Self-Esteem."*

Have You Ever Designed Your Work?

Do you belong to the TGIM (Thank God It's Monday) Club or do you belong to the TGIF (Thank God It's Friday) Club? Do you belong to the IHTW (I Hate to Work) Club or the ILTW (I Love to Work) Club?

Research shows that 85% of Americans are unfulfilled at work. These individuals frequently seek fulfillment outside of the work place. Answer the following questions and give yourself a work checkup.

What is your work? Did you choose your work with a specific purpose in mind? How does your work relate to the outcomes of your office, department or to your self-employed status? What do you like least about your work? What do you like most about your work? How would you like your work to be changed? How would you like management to treat you? What rewards do you get from your work besides money? Example of rewards may be: career development, a career mentor, personal development, friendships, sociability or a sense of purpose.

What is your definition of *service?* How do you serve the public, customers, clients, co-workers or associates? Does your work require *helping people?* Do you help customers, clients or associates? Is there anyone at work who needs your help? Do you need help from anyone? Will you accept the help others are willing to offer? Describe an example of when you have helped someone. If not at work—where?

Describe yourself. Who are you? What are you like? How well do you know yourself? What are your likes and dislikes? Do you know what you value? Can you describe your *feelings* and thoughts? If you had only six months to live, would you change anything in your life? What would you do? What do you want to leave behind to grow? What are your main satisfactions in life, both inside and outside of work?

Name three people, living or dead, you most admire. What are your reasons for admiring them? What have you done to develop yourself? What does self-development mean to you? Do you get any help in developing yourself? Can you recall when and how you became interested in self-development? How would you like to develop yourself in and outside of work? Do you believe your present work could further your outcomes of self-development? What is your vision of the kind of person you would like to become? What is your ultimate ideal career?

I encourage you to answer these questions and design a work plan **and then, watch what happens!**

"*I now design my work the way I want it.*"

Do You Have A Personal Marketing Plan?

Do you have a personal marketing plan for your career? Who needs a marketing plan? Everyone! If you don't know where you are going, you will probably end up somewhere else! You need a marketing plan to sell products, services, ideas and above all—yourself. A concise marketing plan will allow you to focus your time and energy in one direction, thereby increasing your effectiveness.

You need to market yourself every day. A marketing plan is a conscious organized written tool. It describes your present career situation, opportunities and challenges. It notes specific and realistic career outcomes. The marketing plan also outlines specific action steps required to accomplish these outcomes, including a milestone chart.

Career marketing planning is a continuous process. Develop a one sentence definition of what you have to offer or want to offer the world. This may also be known as your statement of purpose or mission statement. Do your best to limit it to 12 words or less—ideally five to nine words. Be sure to make your one sentence marketing plan specific, realistic and written in the present tense, while still focusing on the future you want to create.

For example, my statement is, "I am a Self-Esteem Consultant creating Global Self-Esteem." My extended version is, "I am a Self-Esteem Consultant offering speaking, seminars and consulting services to business and the general public to create Global Self-Esteem."

To take this a step further, you want to create a support system to obtain the outcomes of your personal marketing plan. Draw a line down the center of a blank piece of paper. On the left side, list the things you do not want in your career. On the right side, list the things you do want. On another sheet of paper, list the components of your ultimate ideal career and work situation.

Now you are ready to establish your career milestones. For example, you may want to earn $1 million in the next 5, 10 or 15 years, work in Europe, publish a book or own your own business. You can accomplish any outcome as long as you are willing to do what it takes to implement it. Prepare a 5, 10 and 15 year milestone chart. Write the outcomes you want. Include the dates on which you want to achieve the outcomes and the rewards you will give yourself. Be flexible to accept and rearrange your pathway as you have new insights.

Take all of this information and create affirmations to support your milestones and personal marketing plan. Remember to make them personal, present tense and seven to nine words. Verbalize these affirmations with *feelings* three times a day. Say them once in the morning, once in the afternoon and once right before going to sleep. Visualize reaching each of your milestones and obtaining your ultimate ideal career and work situation.

Finally, make the commitment to vitalize, that is take action on, your affirmations **and then, watch what happens!**

> *"I now commit to my personal*
> *marketing plan."*

What Do You Know About Interviewing?

When was the last time you interviewed for a job or career position? Are you comfortable during these interviews? Do you know how to ask questions to obtain the outcome you want? Are you aware that an interview is two-sided? A company is looking at you and you are looking to see if the company is ideal for you.

Below are some questions that I originally gave to the students in my "Orientation to Business" class at the University of Cincinnati. I continually receive great feedback, both from the students and organizations. They found the interviewing process to be more refreshing and unique because the interviewee was asking questions of the interviewer.

You can ask these questions, as an interviewer or interviewee, to obtain your ultimate ideal position either as an employee or business owner. I suggest you interview at least

25 companies or people before making a final decision about the position or person.

Up-Front Information (Acquire before the interview.)

1. How large is the company or organization?
2. What are the company's assets?
3. How long has it been in business?
4. How diversified are its products or services?
5. What kind of reputation does the company have locally?—nationally?—internationally?
6. What kind of management structure does the company have?
7. What is the nature of the company's business?
8. Is the company in a period of growth, and what are its prospects for growth?
9. Are there trends that cause the business to fluctuate: weather, technology, economics?
10. What are the fringe benefits?
11. Will traveling be required?
12. What is the company's debt load?

What to look for in the Interviewee or Interviewer

1. Does he or she know the men and women in his/her field?
2. Is he or she credible?
3. Is he or she articulate?
4. Does he or she listen?
5. Does he or she ask incisive questions?
6. Does he or she convey a sense of purpose?
7. Does he or she create a favorable impression?

As the Interviewer, you may want to ask the Interviewee (This will give you general qualities that may be advantageous for a particular position.)

1. What is your background?
2. What are your skills?
3. What are your hobbies?

Suggested Questions as Interviewer and Interviewee (All questions need to be properly placed and appropriately paced. The questions with a * need to be asked after rapport has been established. They help you discover Prime Movers.)

1. Tell me about yourself.
2. Tell me about your company/organization.

3. What is happiness for you?
4. How would you describe your energy level?
5. Do you have a mentor?
6. What are your greatest skills?
7. What does "the good life" mean to you?
8. Trace your career path from college to the present time.
9. What are your top five priorities?
10. What is the latest date you have decided to retire?
11. What does success mean to you?
12. What do you like best about your current job? (or last job?)
13. What do you like least about your current job? (or last job?)
14. What would you like to change?
15. Do you exercise regularly?
16. What are your company's/organization's goals?
17. What are your personal goals?
18. What death issue (something that causes the reduction or death of a company) has your company/organization faced this year?
19. Do you take regular vacations?
20. How is your health?
21. Do you participate in community activities?
22. What qualities do you like best in an employee? (employer?)
23. What do you like best about yourself?
24. What would you like to look back on as your greatest success?
25. Have you planned the rest of your life?
26. How many dead-end jobs are in the company/organization?
*27. How effective are you now?
*28. How much of your own money have you invested in your personal development in the past twelve months and for what specific purpose?
*29. How do you evaluate your effectiveness?
*30. Where do you want to be positioned in the future in terms of responsibilities and rewards?

*31. Do you get the support you need for the things you want to do?
*32. What use are you making of your knowledge about yourself?
*33. What is your attitude towards responsibilities, risks and rewards?
*34. What was your biggest failure?

As an interviewee, remember to ask how long the interview will be and then use half of the time to ask your own questions. How you are treated during an interview will give you an idea of how you will be treated when employed or associated with that person or business. Don't settle for less! You deserve the best!

I encourage you to use these questions in the interviewing process to obtain the person or position you want **and then, watch what happens!**

> *"I now ask incisive questions during the interviewing process."*

"Create Elegant, Exquisite and Irresistible Outcomes!"

Quote by William J. McGrane, CPAE

Chapter Nine

Your Social Life

How Involved Are You In Your Community?

Have you ever heard the name Kitty Genovese? Many years ago, she was driving home from work at 3:20 a.m. in the neighborhood of Queens, New York. She parked her car and then walked toward her apartment. In the darkness Miss Genovese noticed a stranger. She sensed something and began walking quickly toward a police call box to summon help. She got as far as a street lamp when a man grabbed her.

Her screams cut through the night. She cried, "Oh my God, he stabbed me. Please help me! Please help me!" Lights went on. Someone called down, "Let that girl alone." It was just the beginning of Miss Genovese's horrible death.

According to the police report, the killer left when the lights went on; however, he returned when they went out and stabbed her again. Again she screamed. Again lights went on. The killer fled, yet returned a third time to inflict the fatal wounds as Miss Genovese lay slumped at the door of an apartment building where she crawled for safety.

Listen carefully to the point of this story. During the 35 minute ordeal, 38 people watched or heard all or part of the attack. One couple later said they turned their lights out and moved closer to get a better view. At 3:50 a.m., a man called the police and said, "I did not want to get involved!"

I have told that story many times during my speaking career. I have a vivid memory of that event of the late 1960's. What is the reason I am sharing the story with you?

Psychologists and psychiatrists have wondered, "How come Americans remember that tragedy so well?" The public was shocked at both the seriousness of the act and the apathy of the bystanders. The lack of responsibility for a fellow human being in trouble was alarming. However, the professionals learned that people do not want to get involved.

Some of the statements from the 38 people included the following.

"Frankly we thought it was a lover's quarrel."

"We were afraid."

"I was tired."

Can it happen again? The answer is "yes," as long as the Self-Esteem of the observers is not intact. We all need to create a safe environment where people can thrive. This can be accomplished when we each take responsibility for everything we think, say, do and *feel.*

Decide now to take action by being involved in your community crime watch program **and then, watch what happens!**

> *"I now choose to get involved in my community crime watch program."*

How Are Your Communication Skills?

When was the last time you evaluated your communication skills? How often do you upgrade your vocabulary? Check, starting now, on the quality of your speech. What words do you use to get the best possible outcomes with all of your interpersonal relationships? Notice how often conflict and misunderstanding creates violence and broken friendships because of the words we use to describe our *feelings.*

Your words and your voice trigger all kinds of *feelings.* It is happening to you now. You have specific *feelings* about this message on communication. Next, observe your voice. Your voice has power. *The way you use your voice is an indication of your Self-Esteem and the degree of your personal power.* So use your soft voice, your normal voice and your command voice when it is appropriate. People will be more likely to listen to you. They will also be more likely to *feel* comfortable around you. If they know they will be affirmed by you every time they meet you, they may want to be your friend. It is important to value the power of your vocabulary and how you use your voice to create a climate of acceptance with every person you meet.

Another communication skill is listening. Pretend you are hearing rather then reading this message. How would you be listening to this message? Would you be giving the ideas your undivided attention? Are you aware of the way you listen to people? Have you noticed that when your Self-Esteem is intact, you are a better listener?

If you want the best relationships with your children, spouse and in fact, everyone—*learn to listen to everyone as if they are the most important person in your world at that moment.* Be totally focused on that person, ignoring all distractions.

Next, are you convinced that your body language is a powerful communication skill? The way you stand and sit, your body movement, as well as your eye contact affects the *feeling* tone you create with each person, which influences your message in a unique way.

Start now to observe your voice, your words, your body language, and finally your communication skill of touch. Yes, touch has more power than words. Research has shown that untouched infants do not thrive or survive. The human touch has a comforting power. It's very important that we each receive this touch on a daily basis. There are many acceptable ways to accomplish this.

Touch someone today with a handshake, a pat on the back or even a hug **and then, watch what happens!**

> *"I now upgrade my vocabulary, voice, listening, body language and touching communication skills."*

Are Conversation Skills Important?

Have you read the book *What Do You Say After You Say Hello?* by Eric Berne? Do you find creating a stimulating in-depth conversation challenging, or is it easy for you? When you were a child, did your parents read to you? Did you read to your parents? Do you love to read now? Does your family love to read?

I fell in love with reading after graduate school. More than 50,000 new books are published every year, not counting textbooks. And yet, 80 million Americans are illiterate to some degree.

What are the consequences of poor reading skills and an inadequate vocabulary? Is it possible that these people are also lacking in conversation skills? Do you believe that violence may be the result of the inability to describe *feelings*? Have you noticed people who freeze when they are part of a group? They just stand and listen and *feel* like they are dying inside because they are not sure how to participate in conversations.

Philosopher George Herbert said, "He who can speak well can command what he wants." George Howe in his book, *The Miracle of Dialogue* says, "Communication means life or death to persons." Could talk TV and radio shows be the outlet for people who want to observe conversation rather than participate? *Conversation is the act of communicating our thoughts, feelings, beliefs and ideas to ourselves and others.* It is one of the principal ways we connect with one another. We usually converse by making statements or asking questions. Very often, statements are taken at face value and internalized without question. Whereas, questions can stimulate the thinking and *feeling* process.

What is the reason I am sharing this kind of message with you? It is because many people have told me they do not know how to carry on meaningful conversations. They *feel* uncomfortable and awkward which diminishes their Self-Esteem. One of the skills I teach is superlative communication through the Art of Asking Questions.

It is important to learn to ask questions of ourselves and others so we can discover what we or they need, want and value. Questions can be asked with manipulation, exploitation, or integrity. People with intact Self-Esteem learn to ask questions with integrity (honesty). We have the other person's best interest at heart. The question we always need to be considering is, "What question can help this person discover what he needs, wants and values?"

Aside from developing intact Self-Esteem, I believe, that conversational skills are the most important skills needed to have a happy home, a rewarding social life and a successful career.

Upgrade your conversation skills daily **and then, watch what happens!**

> **"I now invest in my conversation skills."**

What Does The Statue of Liberty Mean To You?

How do you *feel* about the Statue of Liberty? It took 100 years before it was refurbished. Many people donated money to preserve the statue. Are you an American? If so, do you *feel* privileged to be an American? The Statue of Liberty is a symbol of freedom. For many people coming to the United States, it was the first evidence they saw that they had reached their cherished destination. What does the symbol mean to you? Here is what it means to me.

S – Stands for *Self-Esteem*. The freedom to *feel* respect for myself. The freedom to release all of my potential when I choose to do so.

Y – Represents a *yearning* for happiness and fulfillment which may be different for each person.

M – Stands for the *meaning* we put into the seven areas of our life: Spiritual, Mental, Financial, Social, Physical, Family and Career to experience a balanced lifestyle.

B – Represents the *behavioral* choices we make to preserve our freedom and to create mutually beneficial relationships. With intact Self-Esteem, we are free of distress, and we create harmony and peace of mind wherever we go. We help people to *feel* better about themselves all the time.

O – Stands for *opportunity*. In America we choose what we want to do, we decide where we will live, we say what we want and we worship as we wish.

L – Represents *Lifelong Learning* to be free of criticism, blame, guilt, punishment and value judging. It means I value myself enough to be a beacon (an inspiration) to everyone I meet.

The Statue of Liberty is a symbol of T.U.A. (Total Unconditional Acceptance) for all people from all over the world. With T.U.A., comes freedom. It is the freedom to develop all of your potential, to discover your skills and abilities, to travel, to speak about what is on your mind and heart and to BE all that you can BE. Freedom is accompanied by responsibility. A well known psychologist, William Glasser, defines responsibility as, "The ability to fulfill one's needs, and to do so in a way that does not deprive others of the ability to fulfill their needs." I personally agree with Dr. Glasser and believe that there is no freedom without accepting responsibility for everything you think, say, do and *feel*.

From now on use the symbol of the Statue of Liberty as your guide **and then, watch what happens!**

> *"I now cherish the symbol of the Statue of Liberty as a reminder of my commitment to give T.U.A. to everyone."*

How Can You Be An Interesting Conversationalist?

How many interesting conversations have you had today, this week or this year? How many have you had in your lifetime? What is an interesting conversation to you? Is it only when someone makes you the center of attention?

Some people are superlative communicators. Others may be hungry to learn the Art of Conversation. Who listens to you as you talk about your ideas, *feelings* and interests? Who do you listen to? We have a tendency to listen to someone who first is interested in us. Then we find it is easier to listen to them.

The television and the computer have influenced our personal and professional interaction dramatically. All skills take practice—practice—practice. Planning and preparation are the keys to any success. I believe 95% of personal and career success is the result of our communication skills. The foundation of our communication skills is our Self-Esteem. How can you improve your conversation competence?

First: *Develop a powerful vocabulary.* Words are tools. You have to verbally communicate what thoughts and *feelings* are going on inside of you. Learn a new word every day. Write it five times and then put the word into a sentence. You can add 365 new words to your vocabulary each year with this process.

Second: *Develop your voice so people are comfortable listening to you.* Notice the qualities of the voices you like. Decide to cultivate your voice. Speak into a tape recorder and discover the nuances in your speech that can be improved. Sing your favorite songs in the shower and read out loud. This will help you to add color and style to your speaking voice.

Third: *Be aware of your body language.* Are you aware of your facial expressions? What are your facial expressions saying to the person? Are they congruent with what you want to communicate? How is the positioning of your body affecting you and the person in front of you? Do you have open or closed body posture? Are you having eye contact? Do you give each person your undivided attention?

It is important to avoid the conversation errors of interrupting and stepping on people's sentences before they finish. Remember, communication power is: 7% words, 38% tone of voice, and 55% body language. Upgrade, refine and develop these three areas. Take one new action a day. Make it easy. As you layer these actions, day after day, you will be surprised at the skills you acquire in 3, 6 and 12 months.

Above all—enjoy your conversations, have fun **and then, watch what happens!**

> *"I now choose to be an interesting conversationalist."*

How Do You Use Your Voice?

Do you remember the "And then Some Principle" (do what you are paid to do "And Then Some")? What does the "And Then Some Principle" have to do with how you use your voice?

Remember the last time you talked with someone on the phone? You may have needed to ask for help, obtain information or solve an issue. Maybe you wanted to return something or learn more about their products or services. Do you remember the voice? How would you describe it? How did you *feel?* Was the "And Then Some Principle" being used with you? How could you tell? Do you believe that individual also experienced *feelings* in response to your voice?

The next time you call your favorite store, notice the tone of voice of the person who answers the phone. Are they pleased that you called? Observe how long it takes you to get an answer or solution to your question or concern. Hear the words the person uses to communicate with you. Listen for courtesy, concern and enthusiasm! That's the "And Then Some Principle."

Focus on your telephone skills. If someone were evaluating your telephone competence, would they recommend you for a raise or a promotion? Would they say you have the "And Then Some Principle" in your voice? Your voice has the power to turn people on or turn them off. Basically you have three voices. You can use a soft voice, your normal voice or a command voice. Each is appropriate based on the circumstances and the outcome you want to receive.

When you listen to a speaker, watch television or go to a movie, observe the power of each voice. How does it create an impact on you? Do you want to listen longer or do you want to turn them off?

Recall the voices from your past. Whose do you remember? What voices helped to make you *feel* comfortable? How come? Were there voices you *felt* uncomfortable hearing? Do you still have a dislike of certain voice tones? Do these voices remind you of anyone or anything? How does this affect your relationships? Have you ever heard the "And Then Some Principle" in a voice? It may have been someone using your name or giving you an affirmation. It could be the way someone asks you a question. Did they sound interested in what you were saying? Did they seem to have an attitude of service?

Decide now to develop your voice to create a climate of acceptance. Refuse to yell or scream at anyone. Use your voice appropriately, based on the situation. Soften your voice whenever anyone is upset or angry. Develop the many ranges of your normal voice so people identify the "And Then Some Principle."

For the next week invest in improving your voice **and then watch what happens!**

> *"I now soften my voice to create a climate of acceptance."*

Have You Reviewed Your Conversational Skills?

Do you watch television? Do you watch television talk shows? If so, who is your favorite talk show personality? There are more than 500 talk shows. How come people like to watch talk shows? How much television do you watch? Are you aware that the average American watches television at least seven hours daily? Do you notice the topics that attract your attention?

Have you heard that many people have difficulty describing their *feelings?* Conversation is one of the key ways to describe and release *feelings.* How would you evaluate your conversational skills? Here are some questions to answer. How well do you communicate verbally? How large is your vocabulary? What does your body language say? Do you like to touch, to hug? Were you hugged when you were a child? Are you open to new ideas? Do you know your natural conversation style? What are your values? When was the last time you wrote down your values as they relate to communicating with people?

Where do you invest your energy? Does your energy decrease or increase when you have a conversation with someone? How come? How would you define a mutually beneficial relationship? What are your relationship skills? Do you compare yourself with others (which is a form of self-image behavior)?

Is your Self-Esteem intact? In other words, how much do you respect yourself? Are you aware of how you *feel* about yourself? Can you describe these *feelings*? What are your attitudes about life and conversations? How much time do you invest in conversation with people daily? How often do you initiate conversations? Do you take advantage of every opportunity to carry on a conversation with people?

To increase your conversational knowledge it is important to first learn about yourself. Keep a journal to write your *feelings* about your needs, wants and values. Second, read books about communication skills. Third, listen to educational audio cassette tapes on communication, conversations and relationships. Fourth, observe others, especially those who are excellent conversationalists. Become aware of the skills you want to learn and the progress you are making.

Now is the time to practice your conversational skills. Begin by initiating conversations. Take small steps. In the beginning, talk with people for a maximum of five minutes. Discover three new pieces of information about them that you never knew. Then create conversations that last ten, fifteen and twenty minutes.

Upgrade your conversation skills **and then, watch what happens!**

> *"I now improve my conversation skills daily."*

What Is A Servant Leader?

Have you ever voted for a President? How did you make your decision? Did you vote the way your parents did? What are your major concerns for the USA and the world? Do you believe that the major skill all Presidents need is leadership?

The best simple definition of a leader is someone who has followers! Historically, many of us are familiar with the consequences of Stalin, Hitler and all of the world leaders as well as all Presidents of the United States. Because of the potential of a nuclear holocaust, I believe we now need a true servant leader. Robert K. Greenleaf, author of *Servant Leadership*, says, "A servant leader is servant first then a leader second."

My first recommendation to a leader is to develop intact Self-Esteem and model Self-Esteem behavior for the world. Leaders with intact Self-Esteem are servants. We need servant leaders in families, government, business, education, health care and spiritual groups.

How can you identify a servant leader? A servant leader leads through the influence of his or her example. Walt Whitman answered this when he wrote, "We convince by our presence." Servant leaders help other people meet their highest priority needs. The best test of a servant leader, as well as the most difficult to administer, is to ask these questions: Do those served grow as people? During the process of being served, do these people become healthier, wiser and freer? Are those being served more autonomous (self-directing) and are they more likely to become servants? What effect is the leader having on the less privileged in society? Will these individuals benefit or at least not suffer additional deprivation?

All leaders have outcomes. The servant leader creates trust in their outcomes. Followers recognize that the servant leader serves with integrity by helping them discover their own outcomes. Leaders do not elicit trust unless they have intact Self-Esteem and reflect this in their values and competence. They also need to have a driving force that will support the tenacious pursuit of an outcome regardless of obstacles encountered. Not much happens without a dream.

Behind every great achievement is a dreamer of great dreams. However, it takes much more than just a dreamer to bring dreams into reality. The dream, of course, has to be there first. Then, because of commitment and effort, the servant leader acts with integrity to bring the dream into reality.

Elect a servant leader **and then, watch what happens.**

> *"I now choose a servant leader to lead us to freedom and world peace."*

What Is Networking?

When you hear the word "network," what do you think? Is it radio or television network? Is it a network of friends, family or business associates? What about the work connection? Does that mean a peer connection, a mentor connection or a career connection?

Now what about the word "feedback"? Does that mean telling members of your family how much you appreciate them? Does feedback mean giving your children specific affirmations about their value and skills, as well as paying attention to their interests? Does feedback mean staying in touch with important people in your life by creating a network of significant others and connecting with them? Some of the ways you can do that are by:

1. Writing to people.
2. Calling people.
3. Giving gifts.
4. Meeting people face to face.
5. Visiting people on a regular basis.
6. Being open to new relationships.
7. Increasing your flexibility.
8. Exploring a larger you.
9. Releasing past resentments.
10. Forgiving all hurts
11. Appreciating different beliefs.

12. Beginning again.
13. Clarifying your desires and values.
14. Choosing to connect and network daily.
15. Making agreements and commitments and keeping them.
16. Allowing for playfulness.
17. Taking action, however small.
18. Enjoying self expression and conversation.
19. Listening with alert compassion.
20. Being open to adventure and fun.
21. Discovering your inner resources.
22. Developing your Self-Esteem skills daily.
23. Increasing your range of choices by considering more options in your life.

Decide now to build your own network of family and others in an intact Self-Esteem way.

Make deep connections and give specific feedback **and then, watch what happens!**

> *"I now create a network of connections with family and others and give them frequent specific feedback."*

How Are You At Conversing With Others?

What is the most important topic of conversation for you today? Is it your career, relationships, health or children? Are you talking about the quality of education in your community? Have you been discussing world conditions? Do you have discussions on books, TV programs, movies, sports, travel, career or success? Do you have a discussion club where you share ideas important to you? Are you comfortable conversing when you attend a dinner or party? What level of competence do you have as a conversationalist?

This week, observe your own conversations and those of other people around you. The Art of Conversation is a special skill that needs a lifetime of development. In the first two minutes, when you meet someone, you basically have three topics to choose from: the situation or event, the other person or yourself. And there are only three ways to begin a conversation: ask a question, give your opinion or state a fact. The major outcome in the beginning is just to interest or involve the other person. I believe the best way to start a conversation is by asking a question because it focuses the energy on the other person.

It is important to learn the Art of Conversation and how to ask questions. One of the greatest fears of many people is the fear of being in a group where they know no one. Many people are shy or afraid of being rejected. They do not know how to begin a conversation. However, with practice and skill, people can learn to be comfortable in any situation.

Dr. Phillip Zimbardo, author of *Shyness: What Is It, What To Do About It*, says 85 million people wake up every day with some degree of shyness. Millions of people buy animals and plants because it is easier to talk to animals and plants rather than talk to people. People talk back. Animals and plants "listen."

Decide now to upgrade your conversation skills. Learn to ask questions, listen externally, give eye contact and give each person your undivided attention. Learn something about everything, and everything you can about something. This will give you a knowledge base for asking questions. You can go to everyone's "school" by asking them questions about their skills and interests. As you develop the Art of Conversation and release any of your fears and shyness, you will also be letting people know about you.

Take an interest in others, ask questions **and then, watch what happens!**

> *"I now continually refine my conversation skills."*

Have You Heard Of People Reading?

Do you like to read books? Would you be interested in learning about a new kind of reading, People Reading? Now may be the time for you to reach out to new experiences. You have opportunities every day to meet new people, share ideas and develop new and more meaningful relationships. These are also times to test your conversation skills.

Your unintact or intact Self-Esteem determines how difficult or how easy it is for you to talk with people. This includes your conversations with those you do not know as well as those people you do know. Take a moment now to review your day.

How were your conversations? Do you greet everyone you meet with enthusiasm and high energy? That is what I notice first when I meet a person. What is their energy level? Are they genuinely interested in me? Are they comfortable with themselves? Do they like themselves? Are they shy? What can I do to bring out the best in them? All of these questions can be answered with the skill of People Reading.

Everyone is *interesting* to the degree they are *interested*. The person they are most interested in is themselves. This is human nature. The more I know myself, the easier it is to speak to and focus on other people. To People Read, I need to be aware that everyone is a "book." Their personal history is filled with great life experiences, and I would like to learn about them. Many people only read the cover or, at most, the table of contents. To receive the greatest gifts, I encourage you to read the entire book. This can only be done with the skill of People Reading.

The first skill in People Reading is the Art of Asking Questions. Without questions, it is difficult to open anyone's book. Then you can learn the second most valuable skill in People Reading—the Art of External Listening. With these two skills, you can begin a meaningful conversation. You can give each person your undivided attention, be patient, avoid finishing sentences and wait for them to complete their thoughts. Listen for their hot buttons. A hot button is something they love to talk about, i.e., a topic which makes them most alive. By using their words, you can proceed to ask them questions and discover chapter after chapter of their lives.

Invest today in People Reading. See how long you can keep a conversation going. Listen to what they say to you when you stop talking. You may create a "WOW!" experience where they say, "That was the most interesting conversation I ever had. I can't wait to see you again!" The key is, they did most of the talking. With People Reading, you can receive more energy, create new friends and develop your Self-Esteem.

Take action now by reading five new people every day and **then, watch what happens!**

> **"I now People Read five new people a day."**

Are You Tithing Your Talents?

Do you volunteer some of your time to an organization? George Gallup, the forecaster of the future, says that a tremendous number of Americans are now involved in volunteer work. This force of free labor could provide the springboard for far-reaching political and social change in the next two decades. The Gallup Poll recently did an extensive study on volunteerism in America, and it was discovered that 52% of adults and 53% of teenagers had volunteered to do some kind of work without receiving any pay.

Many people volunteer at Rotary Club, Kiwanis, Big Brothers, Big Sisters or nursing homes. Some teach reading and math skills or help such organizations as the American Cancer Society, the Heart Association, the Red Cross or the Nutrition Council. The largest percent of volunteers are involved in religious activities. Nineteen percent of the adult volunteers and 20% of the teenagers work at churches. The next largest areas of volunteer work are health care and education. These volunteers do fundraising, hospital work, serving the rescue squad, working with the elderly, helping the Parent-Teacher Association, contributing to school board service and tutoring.

Current research shows that people from the middle and upper income levels are most likely to volunteer. Sixty-three percent of volunteers had an annual income of $24,000.00 or more. The reason most commonly given for volunteering by both adults and teens is that they wanted to do something useful to help others.

When people *feel* they can make a difference, they are more likely to get involved. How about you? Do you tithe 10% of your talent to an organization you believe in? What are your top five skills that may serve an organization? Do you have any hobbies that can be volunteered? Is there a cause bigger than life that you are interested in furthering? Look in all seven areas of your life to discover where you can be a volunteer: Spiritual, Mental, Financial, Social, Physical, Family or Career.

I believe that people who give themselves away, who volunteer their skills, are more fulfilled, freer from loneliness, have more friends and contribute to the preservation of the American sense of service to others. Decide now to contact your favorite service organization.

Tithe 10% of your talent **and then, watch what happens!**

> *"I now tithe 10% of my talent because*
> *I can make a difference."*

Are You Complimenting People?

Has anyone criticized you lately? How do you *feel* when someone puts you down or criticizes your work or your actions? Do you fight? Do you flee? Do you stay and communicate and ask for your missing piece (that which is absent from your life—be it a need, want or value)?

Many people love to criticize other people. Critics define the world through their eyes. They want to be general managers of the world. Criticism only creates fear, pain, distress and more criticism. I once heard the newly elected president of a large service organization speak. Part of his remarks included this statement, "I do not give out many compliments to people." He continued by saying, "In fact I spent one year trying to find something about the previous president that I could criticize. I could not find anything."

My suggestion to him is to invest his next year, as president, in giving at least one compliment a day. Then when his year is up and he tallies up his achievements, he can report that he gave a minimum of 365 genuine compliments to a minimum of 365 people.

In all of my presentations I always ask the audience, "How many of you have had enough compliments and recognition in your life?" No one ever raises his or her hand. People want to receive more compliments and recognition. Have you ever wondered about the reason it is so difficult to give compliments or receive compliments? The answer is very simple. If you have not been complimented, then it is difficult to give compliments. Would you like to change that? May I suggest you read a book called *Warm Fuzzies and Cold Pricklies* by Dana Joel. It is about a beautiful little valley surrounded by mountains. People there lived a happy life. They gave and received compliments which they called "warm fuzzies."

What would the world be like if people received genuine compliments every day? This week declare your independence from criticism, put downs, sarcasm and verbal abuse. *Feel* free to give compliments to at least one person for the next 365 days. A year from now review and add up the number of fuzzies you gave to people and the number you received. Start complimenting now **and then, watch what happens!**

> *"I now give one compliment to*
> *at least one person a day."*

How Do You *Feel* About Violence?

How do you *feel* about the amount of violence in the world? What can you do to eliminate such violence? Just what is the meaning behind such violence?

Please read and then react to this statement. "All violence is a request for love, acceptance, personal power, inclusion, recognition and attention." How do you *feel* about that?

As I became aware of my own unintact Self-Esteem behavior, I discovered my major act of violence was verbal. I used words because words have power and create *feelings* as people interpret the meanings. Words can show love, encouragement or some degree of violence. Until I developed my Self-Esteem, my mouth and the words I used had the potential to cause others to hurt. Then I learned a shocking truth—"I only attempt to hurt others to the degree I am personally hurting!" I can only give what I have.

All violence is a request to *feel* like a somebody. If you *feel* like a nobody and you want to *feel* like a somebody, then you may do your best to put others down, to make them *feel* like a nobody, so you can be a somebody. This is violence and it can become a habit. After repeating this behavior over and over you become numb to your *feelings*.

Verbal and physical violence is epidemic in the world. What can you do about it? First you need to develop your Self-Esteem. You need to learn that Self-Esteem is different from self-image. Self-image is a imitation or representation of what you want to present to the world. It is comparison and it destroys Self-Esteem.

Self-Esteem is the self respect you feel for yourself. You can recognize your Self-Esteem by your behavior. When you are respectful of yourself and others, then you know your Self-Esteem is intact. The words you use can help you in developing your Self-Esteem as well as that of others.

So read books, listen to cassette tapes and attend learning programs to upgrade your vocabulary. Then you can choose Self-Esteem language especially when your Self-Esteem is challenged. With intact Self-Esteem you can learn to: be patient, respect your own point of view, listen to and respect other people's points of view, ask questions, soften your voice and avoid all criticism and put downs of yourself and others. If you could give one gift to the world to deal with the violence, I suggest it be the gift of Self-Esteem.

Begin by giving the gift of Self-Esteem to yourself first **and then, watch what happens!**

> *"I now build a Self-Esteem vocabulary*
> *to avoid violence."*

Do You Have High Energy?

Do you have high energy now? Do you know people who have low energy? Are there times when your energy is low? What do you think creates low or high energy? How does your energy level influence your career and relationships? Would you believe that people are always aware (consciously or unconsciously) of your energy, your enthusiasm, your excitement about life?

The instant test is when you meet a person. In the first two minutes your energy towards that person is determined by your Self-Esteem. When your Self-Esteem is intact, your energy will be high. Your energy will be low when your Self-Esteem is not intact.

In her book *Energy*, Naura Hayden asks these six questions.

1. Are you a victim of the human energy crisis?
2. Are you drained at the end of the day and sometimes at the beginning of the day?
3. Are you tired a lot?
4. Do you drink a lot of coffee to rev up your motor?
5. Do you smoke lots of cigarettes because they give you the lift you need?
6. Do you drink alcohol during the lunch hour and a couple more at night?

Ms. Hayden says, "If you answer 'yes' to any one of these questions and *feel* you need any kind of pill to take you up or down, then you are a victim of the human energy crisis."

Most of us have heard about energy shortages: gas, oil, coal and electricity. Yet, the most important energy is the one that runs our personal motors. This energy gives us a zest for living; one that lets us absorb life's challenges and keep on going with a smile, knowing that nothing can keep us down.

The best way I know to keep your energy high is to energize your Self-Esteem every day. I believe energy is everything. Energy is great health. Energy channeled with intact Self-Esteem will get you anything you want: love, friendship, money, power, fun, success—everything!

Decide now to mix yourself a daily Self-Esteem energy milkshake **and then, watch what happens!**

"I now choose high energy behavior daily."

Afterword

A Son's Love For His Dad

Sunday July 18, 1993
3:35 PM
Room 834
Dallas, Texas
Sheraton Suites

Just got back from the 20th anniversary celebration of the National Speakers Association and *felt* I needed to process my feelings around these years.

What is really creating a lot of *feelings* is seeing the 20 year history book. It goes back to the first convention I attended in 1975 in Phoenix, Arizona when Bob, Mom, Dad and I were together. Here I am, 18 years later in my own room, alone. Mom had the opportunity to go to Europe. Miriam does not *feel* the need to continue being at these conventions.

I am flooded with all the *feelings* around my dad inviting me to come on the trip and Dave Yoho inviting me to become a member of the National Speakers Association. Membership in NSA reflects the evolution of my career. There is a picture of my father in the 20 year history book.

I recall all the notes and encouragement he gave me. I really do miss his presence. I *feel* this is a milestone year being here as Bill III. I have no one to depend on and no one to nurture me. It's just me here on my own. We had so much fun on these trips each year. The heat is a real anchor bringing me back to Arizona. It is hard to believe when one era ends and a new one begins. Tonight at 7 to 9 PM I am hosting a *Success Strategies Gathering* for graduates and guests in the Texas area. All the *feelings* of "Take a Bite Out Of Life" come rushing back.

I am sobbing now as I connect with my *feelings* on missing you Dad. I am *feeling* your love and support. I am *feeling* and knowing your belief in me. I am *feeling* your caring and nurturing to make a difference in my life. I am *feeling* your special notes throughout the years and your love.

Yes, all of this T.U.A. (Total Unconditional Love) and encouragement is manifesting itself in this very moment. I am filled with the reality that my greatest mentor is no longer on this earth. These *feelings* create deep pain and at the same time appreciation. Both Dean (my mother) and Bill (my dad) have influenced my destiny forever. Going back to Sugernotch and Wilkes-Barre, Pennsylvania to visit Dad's sister, my Aunt Rita, after fifteen years of being away, really anchored how powerful my father's personal history was and how he modeled moving-on in his life. I recall all the meetings and conventions we attended together. As I cry, tears of agony and pain, I recall my dad saying, "talk through the tears"! Well Dad, I am writing through them.

You have made such a difference in my life and that is filling me in this moment. Your love was so deep. I thank you so much for it. I know it continues to be with me now. I truly feel the umbilical cord is broken in this moment. I am now free to take what helped me to become who I am and flap my own wings as I continue to give myself away.

I miss your face. I miss your eyes. I miss your voice. I miss your hugs. I miss your knowledge. I miss your love. I now know I needed this time alone to grieve your loss and feel the deep love and connection you and I had and continue to have. The "Law of 250" continues. I will impact more then 250 people just as you did Dad. Through the pain of losing you, I know I am healed. You have taught me to stand on my own two feet. I thank you for that. You taught me to own 100 percent of my personal power.

Your gifts are so many. I need this cleansing for my next new beginning. All the years of layering and support are paying off. I can give myself permission to *feel* the *feelings* and not minimize them. I can give myself permission to grieve your loss.

I love you so much Dad! I thank God I can give myself permission to grieve your loss. I love you so much. If I was the only one benefiting from your Pioneering spirit, you have made a difference! Thank you for going through all that you did.

I have received the baton and now I carry it with my own unique style and flair.

These tears are very cleansing. The pain of loss is replaced with unconditional love. The heaviness released a compassion to move forward and take the legacy I have been given. All the listening, all the questions, all the observations come together in me so that I can share myself.

Tonight is the first *Success Strategies Gathering* I conduct on my own with your spirit present. All those who choose to attend are reminders of the legacy you and those before you started. It is a blessing to carry the torch. It is time for me to take all that I am and be my own person.

Thank you for showing me how. Thank you for caring enough to make a difference in my life. Thank you for your LOVE!!!!!!!!!!!!!!!!!!!!!!!

Your namesake,

Bill McGrane III

Bill McGrane, III

"McGranisms"
by William J. McGrane, CPAE

Life is a series of new beginnings.

Experience the experience of the experience.

Create elegant, exquisite and irrestible outcomes.

Ask for your missing piece.

With intact Self-Esteem you never condone incompetence.

Be present to the moment.

What's more important, the relationship or being right?

Love others into change, not if they change.

Happiness is adjustment.

What do you really, really, really, really, really, really, really want?

Statements destroy communications.

Questions create superlative communication.

Learn something about everything and everything about something.

Create your life the way you want it.

I have a challenge and I need your help.

The choices you make determine the direction of your life.

Appendix

Glossary

Affirm coming from the Latin *affirmare* which means to make firm. To confirm or ratify.

Affirmation is first of all a state of being. "Affirmation comes from the word *affirmare* and means to make firm, to give strength, to make strong. It implies assent, agreement, consent, a willingness to say 'Yes' to all creation. Affirmation is the acceptance of each person as he is." (Thomas A. Kane, author of *The Healing Touch of Affirmation*)

Childlike the retention of youthful characteristics into adult life. Innocent, open, trusting, etc.

Childish silly, infantile behavior such as temper tantrums. Demanding.

Compliment an expression of admiration. To congratulate.

Congruent agreement between your words, feelings and behavior.

Content Oriented being interested in only logical data and information.

Double Looping two people in conversation, each asking questions and responding.

Eureka Moment an "Aha" moment when insight is acquired.

External Listening hearing only what someone is saying without analyzing what they are saying or thinking about how you will reply (internal dialogue).

Finality Statements last comments; nothing more can be added. No room for more information.

Ground bringing an idea into the realm of everyday action. Practical application of an idea or insight.

Incubation gestation, maturation or development of an idea, in-sight, principle, person, etc.

Inner Directed of or pertaining to the mind or spirit. Taking guidance or course of action from within.

Integrity state or quality of honesty, being complete, undivided or unbroken; entirety. It is when what a person thinks, feels, says and does are the same.

Incompletions any unfinished business in your life that keeps emerging or repeating. Often they are around relationships.

214

Intuition the act or process of coming to direct knowledge or certainty without reasoning or rational thought. It is revelation by insight or innate knowledge. Intuition is the direct perception of truth, immediate apprehension and understanding.

Leading the ability to evoke new behavior with other people.

Left Brain the host to language, thinking, facts, figures and the analytical.

Mentor a faithful counselor. A mentor is a resource person who gives direction, accepts you totally and unconditionally, never devalues you through criticism, never tells you what to do or gives you answers or uses guilt, blame or punishment.

Missing Piece that which is absent from your life. A need, want or value.

Neoteny from the Greek words *neos* meaning youth and *teino* meaning to retain. It is the process of growing young, the retention of youthful characteristics in adult life.

Outer Directed taking guidance or course of action from the outside of you. External to you.

Pacing doing something similar to what the other person is doing. You can pace a person's mood, body, speech patterns and phrases.

People Reading asking a person questions for the purpose of getting to know him/her.

Persuasion the act of influencing someone to believe or do something.

    Exploitative to make unfair use of someone or something for one's own advantage or profit.

    Integritive state or quality of being complete, honest, united.

    Manipulative to control the action of.

Plateau Communication rare moments when you are perfectly in tune with another person; communicating with understanding, depth and emotional satisfaction.

Plus adding to.

Process Oriented living life in its continuous change, a continuing development involving many changes.

Right Brain host to motor skills, intuition and emotions.

Self-Disclosure communicating to another person information about yourself that is normally kept hidden.

Self-Esteem the self respect you *feel* for yourself.
   Intact complete and entire.
   Unintact not complete and not entire.

Self-Image an imitation or representation of what you would like to present to the world. It is comparison.

Self-Talk what you say to yourself inside your head.

Toxic Environment poisoned surroundings or conditions.

Unique Factor a special something in a person that threads throughout his/her life.

Value that which is desirable of esteem for its own sake; that which is of importance to an individual.

Value Judging comparing values to find their agreement or disagreement.

Wordsmith a person who gives undivided attention by using the words or languaging of a person, moving forward steadily, yet gradually, to create elegant, exquisite and irresistible outcomes. The master wordsmith tools are: Intact Self-Esteem, The Art of External Listening and The Art of Asking Questions.

Suggested Educational Material
The Institute carries the majority of the suggested products below.

Books:

Born Only Once	by Conrad W. Baars, M.D.
Figuring Kids Out	by Sandra Merwin
How To Live a Good Year Every Year	by Dave Yoho and Jeffrey P. Davidson
How To Raise Your Self-Esteem	by Nathaniel Branden
I Dare You	by William Danforth
Leading Your Sales Team	by Jim Pancero
Living Beyond Fear	by Jeanne Segal, Ph.D.
No Excuse!	by Jay Rifenbary
Peace of Mind at an Early Age	by Grace H. Pilon, SBS
Seven Habits of Highly Effective People	by Steven R. Covey
Six Pillars of Self-Esteem	by Nathaniel Branden
The Choice Is Yours	by Bonnie M. Parsley
The Influence of Fear on Salesmen	by Frank Budd
The Magical Child Within You	by Bruce Davis, Ph.D.
The New People Making	by Virginia Satir
The Nibble Theory	by Kaleel Jamison
The Self-Talk Solution	by Shad Helmstetter
Think and Grow Rich	by Napoleon Hill
Try Giving Yourself Away	by David Dunn

Audio Cassette Albums:

Brighten Your Day With Self-Esteem	by Bill McGrane, CPAE
Celebrate Your Self-Esteem	by Bill McGrane, CPAE
Creating A Self-Esteem Lifestyle	by Bill McGrane, III
It's All Within Your Reach	by Mike Wickett
Leading the Team	by Jim Pancero
No Excuse!	by Jay Rifenbary
Seven Habits of Highly Effective People	by Steven R. Covey
The Art of Asking Questions	by Bill McGrane, III
To Increase Your Sales	by Frank Budd

Posters:

I Am Me	by Virginia Satir
The Tree of Self-Image & Self-Esteem	by Bill McGrane, CPAE

About the McGrane
Self-Esteem Institute

William J. McGrane, CPAE's work continues to flourish through The McGrane Self-Esteem Institute under the direction of his son, Bill McGrane, III.

The McGrane Self-Esteem Institute is a pioneer in the areas of Self-Esteem, Speech and Communications. While our programs are innovative, our mission remains intact: Global Self-Esteem! This is accomplished by providing Self-Esteem, Speech and Communication skills that are tailored to individual's and organization's needs, wants and values.

Public programs offered monthly and bimonthly include:
- *Self-Esteem* (age 18 and up)
- *Psycho-Linguistics* (age 18 and up)
- *Attitudes, Interaction and Achievement* (age 14 & up)
- *Get High On Life with Self-Esteem* (ages 7-13)

If you wish further information on the above programs, other seminars or products of The McGrane Self-Esteem Institute you may contact:

The McGrane Self-Esteem Institute
2055 Dixie Highway, Suite 114
Ft. Mitchell, KY 41011
(606) 341-2216   (800) 341-3304
(606) 341-9634 (fax)

Quantity Sales: *Brighten Your Day With Self-Esteem* in book and cassette album are available at special quantity discounts when purchased in bulk by corporations, organizations and special interest groups. Custom imprinting can also be done to meet specific needs. For details contact:
Success Publishers/Markowski Int'l
One Oakglade Circle
Hummelstown, PA 17036
(717) 566-0468   (717) 566-6423 FAX

McGrane Self-Esteem Foundation

The McGrane Self-Esteem Foundation was established to honor the pioneering work of William J. McGrane, CPAE. His legacy of personal and Global Self-Esteem was what he left behind to grow. His son, Bill McGrane III, followed his father's wish and set up a nonprofit foundation to perpetuate the principles of Global Self-Esteem.

The mission of the McGrane Self-Esteem Foundation is to provide resources and opportunities for individuals to integrate William J. McGrane's philosophies on Global Self-Esteem.

You too can continue the legacy by contributing, sponsoring or recommending the Foundation.

Tax deductible contributions can be made to:
McGrane Self-Esteem Foundation
2055 Dixie Highway, Suite 114
Ft. Mitchell, KY 41011
1-606-341-2216
1-606-341-9634 (fax)

Leaders' Comments (continued from page vi) . . .

"Bill McGrane believed in me from the beginning. He once told me, 'Pat, people are not ready for your special way of speaking because you touch people at their heart. Do not change your way because they all will be coming over to you in the future.' This book speaks from the heart and will touch you in many unexpected ways. You will read it over and over again."

Pat Vivo, CSP
Humorous and Inspirational Speaker
with a Message that Touches Everyone

"Bill McGrane and the powerful ideas in this book have helped me find fulfillment. They are giving me the freedom to be my own person and to have in-depth relationships. Professionally, the principles are allowing me to achieve, accomplish and build layers of trust, resulting in relationships with 'elegant, exquisite and irresistible outcomes.' Take action and you too can live a self-actualizing lifestyle."

Joe Soldano
President
Franklin Graphics Group

"Bill McGrane penetrated my bravado after only a brief meeting. From thereafter, he set me on the path to overcome my hateful insecurities. As a result, he gave me what we all so very fervently desire, INNER PEACE. The reader will achieve the same results long before completing the reading of this book."

Alan Cimberg, CPAE
Speaker specializing in Profitable Salesmanship

"What a wonderful book! This is perhaps the most powerful collection of practical ideas ever written for achieving inner peace, personal effectiveness and high performance. It needs to be read by everyone."

Brian Tracy
Author of *Maximum Achievement*

"If you want to jump start the heart strings of your life and your business, be sure to read William J. McGrane's book *Brighten Your Day With Self-Esteem*. When you read this book you will move your entire life to a whole new level."

Sandy Karn
The Little Entrepreneur With a Big Heart

"This book is loaded with hundreds of powerful ideas, creative insights and Bill McGrane's unique operational examples; growth, development and personal discovery. You will learn new principles for becoming a better parent, teacher, speaker, presenter and person. Read this book and you will bubble with Bill's legacy of life-giving lessons!"

Herb True, PhD
Adjunct Professor of Management
University of Notre Dame

"Magnanimous, robust, vibrant, gentle, sensitive, spiritual, playful and profound best describe William J. McGrane and his work. This awe-inspiring collaboration of a master teacher's philosophy and practical tips will accelerate your path to enlightenment. You will learn integrating tools for embodying success in every aspect of your life. As a trusted friend and colleague of Bill McGrane's, I observed him consistently demonstrating these uplifting principles detailed in the book. With love and high energy, Bill stretched everyone he met on their journey to self-discovery. When I first met Bill in 1979, and shared my exuberance for his self-esteem ideas, he asked, 'Are you ready for the consequences?' Without hesitation I replied, 'YES!' Are you ready for the consequences?"

Patricia Welling, CSP
Midwest Leadership Group
Speaker, Trainer, Consultant

"Bill McGrane was the greatest Self-Esteem teacher and model on earth. His ideas are transforming and have enabled me to create a life of joy and fulfillment that is beyond what I thought was possible. Everyone *needs* to read this book! Just picture the impact of people becoming totally responsible and accepting of self and others. The world immediately becomes a better place because of this book!!!"

Michael Wickett
Michael Wickett International
Speaker, Author, Consultant

"Bill McGrane is the most wise and profound person I have ever met. Read this book, take action with his suggestions and you will know the wisdom of his work."

Jack Canfield, CSP
Self-Esteem Seminars
Bestselling Author of *Chicken Soup For the Soul*

"All of us want richer lives and this book gives us tools to use to make instant progress. Those of us who knew Bill McGrane were made better by his presence and now everyone can learn from his legacy of practical wisdom."

Florence Littauer
President of Class Speakers Inc.
Author of 20 books including *Dare to Dream*

To Hear A "Brighten Your Day" Message

(24 Hours A Day)

Call
1-606-341-9679